Betty Crocker's
New Cake Decorating

Betty Crocker's
New Cake Decorating

Hungry Minds™

Best-Selling Books • Digital Downloads • e-Books • Answer Networks • e-Newsletters • Branded Web Sites • e-Learning

New York, NY ◆ Cleveland, OH ◆ Indianapolis, IN

Hungry Minds, Inc.
909 Third Avenue
New York, NY 10022

For general information on Hungry Minds' products and services, please contact our Customer Care department;
within the U.S. at 800-762-2974, outside the U.S. at 317-572-3993 or fax 317-572-4002.

Library of Congress Cataloging-in-Publication Data

Crocker, Betty
  [New cake decorating]
  Betty Crocker's New Cake Decorating.
      p. cm.
  Rev. ed. of: Betty Crocker's Cake Decorating. ©1990.
  Includes index.
  ISBN 0-02-862527-7
  1. Cake decorating.   I. Title   II. Title: New cake decorating.
TX771.2.C76   1994   93-51020
641.8'653—dc20   CIP

GENERAL MILLS, INC.
Betty Crocker Kitchens
Editor: Lois Tlusty
Recipe Development: Kathleen Eich, Ann E. Stuart
Food Stylists: Cindy Lund, Carol Grones, Connie O'Dell
Photographic Services
Photographer: Nanci Doonan Dixon
Line Drawings: Tina Seeman
Cover Design: Iris Jeromnimon

Manufactured in China
10 9 8 7 6 5 4 3
Second Revised Edition
Front cover: Let's Celebrate Cake (page 60)
Back cover: In-Line Skate Cake (page 36), Fish Cake (page 30)

For consistent baking results, the Betty Crocker Kitchens
recommend Gold Medal Flour.

Contents

Introduction

7

ONE

Cut-Out and Shaped Cakes

9

TWO

Festive Holiday Cakes

51

THREE

Celebration Cakes

83

FOUR

Specialty Bakery Cakes

111

FIVE

Cake Basics

129

Index

155

Introduction

In our fast-paced world, we often think that we don't have the time to create personalized items or add our special brand of whimsy and fun to everyday life. But, with Betty Crocker's *New Cake Decorating*, you'll find that it's possible—and even fun—to make personalized cakes ranging from the formal to the frivolous.

You'll find wonderful new ways to be creative, and most recipes give instructions for both scratch and mix cakes and frostings, so you can decide how best to spend your time.

We think you'll be delighted with the variety of cakes here. For birthdays, there are traditional cut-out designs, such as the Bunny Cake and the Sailboat Cake, but you'll also be amazed at the range of ideas for cakes, whether for birthdays, office parties, family gatherings or other special events. Try the Electric Guitar Cake for a teenager, the Play Ball Cake for a party to celebrate the World Series and the Fish Cake for your favorite angler.

There is an entire chapter on holiday cakes, with beautiful cakes for Christmas, Halloween, Hanukkah and other holidays, including an easy-to-assemble Gingerbread Cake Cottage. Next are "celebration" cakes for specific events, such as weddings, showers and Father's Day. The cakes are highly versatile—use the Computer Cake to celebrate getting the office on-line.

Finally, the section on specialty bakery cakes lets you create stunning cakes that are welcome anytime, such as Lemon Meringue Cake and Decadent Chocolate Cake.

Every cake is photographed, so you'll know exactly how to make it, plus easy-to-follow line drawings make cutting and assembling any cake a stress-free process.

We think once you find out how easy cake decorating can be, you'll be hooked and enjoy making cakes that personalize events, from a friend's birthday to the Spaceship Cake for someone who's "out of this world." Whether you like traditional, whimsical or stunning cakes, you'll find them all right here.

Betty Crocker

Cut-Out and Shaped Cakes

Bunny Cake *10*

Athletic Shoe Cake *11*

Automobile Cake *13*

Ballet Slippers Cake *14*

Bears-on-the-Bus Cake *17*

Bicycle Cake *18*

Big Burger Cake *21*

Cheese and Mouse Cake *22*

Kitty Cat Cake *24*

Snowman Cake *25*

Dinosaur Cake *26*

Electric Guitar Cake *28*

Fish Cake *30*

Gum Ball Machine Cake *32*

Horse's Head Cake *35*

Monkey Cake *36*

In-Line Skate Cake *36*

Panda Cake *38*

Play Ball Cake *40*

Sailboat Cake *43*

Spaceship Cake *44*

Teddy Bear Cake *46*

Train Cake *48*

Bunny Cake (page 10)

IT'S EASY to make "grass" to sprinkle around the bunny. Just shake flaked coconut with a few drops of green food color in a plastic bag.

TIME-SAVER TIP: Substitute 1 package (1 lb 2 oz) carrot cake mix or 1 package (1 lb 2.25 oz) yellow cake mix with pudding for the Carrot Cake. Prepare and bake as directed on package. Substitute 2 tubs (1 lb each) vanilla ready-to-spread frosting for the Creamy White Frosting.

Carrot Cake (page 146)
Creamy White Frosting (page 151)
Tray or cardboard, 20 × 16 inches, covered
Colored sugar
2 white marshmallow-covered chocolate cake balls with creamy filling

Black shoestring licorice
2 large black gumdrops
1 pink licorice candy
1 large red gumdrop
2 pieces candy-coated gum
2 sticks striped fruit-flavored gum

BAKE Carrot Cake as directed for two 8- or 9-inch rounds. Cut one round as shown in diagram. Freeze pieces uncovered about 1 hour for easier frosting if desired. Prepare Creamy White Frosting. Arrange pieces on tray as shown. Frost head and ears with white frosting, attaching pieces with small amount of frosting. Frost bow tie; sprinkle with colored sugar and outline with shoestring licorice.

ARRANGE cake balls on frosting for cheeks. Insert short strips of shoestring licorice into cheeks for whiskers. Outline eyes with shoestring licorice; add short strips for eyelashes. Use black gumdrops for pupils of eyes, pink licorice candy for nose, red gumdrop for mouth and gum for teeth. Cut striped gum into narrow pieces and place in center of ears. Decorate with magician hat and magic wand if desired.

CUTTING AND ASSEMBLING BUNNY CAKE

Cut one layer to form ears and bow tie.

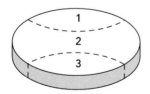

Arrange pieces 1 and 3 atop 4 round layer for ears and piece 2 at bottom for the tie.

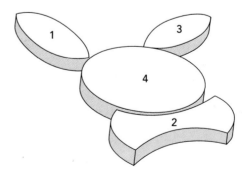

Whole Wheat Applesauce Cake
(page 145)
Creamy White Frosting (page 151)
Tray or cardboard, 14 × 8 inches,
covered
Red paste food color

1 roll grape chewy fruit snack
1 tube (.68 ounce) red decorating
gel, if desired
10 ring-shaped hard candies
Red shoestring licorice

BAKE Whole Wheat Applesauce Cake as directed for 13 × 9-inch rectangle. Cut cake as shown in diagram. Prepare Creamy White Frosting; reserve 1 cup. Place cake piece 1 on tray; frost top with $1/2$ cup frosting. Place piece 2 on top. Trim one end of shoe to form toe as shown in diagram. Attach pieces 3 and 4 on the other end of shoe with small amount of frosting to form high-top opening, trimming to fit and tucking ends of piece 3 inside piece 4. Trim piece 5 and place in high-top opening for tongue. Freeze uncovered about 1 hour for easier frosting if desired. Frost, shaping frosting around piece 5 to resemble tongue. Let frosting set a few minutes. Carefully cover with paper towel and gently pat to give frosting a fabric-like appearance; remove towel.

WRAP base of shoe with fruit snack. Outline desired markings on shoe with toothpick. Tint the reserved frosting red for accent color; fill in markings. Place $1/3$ cup red frosting in decorating bag with writing tip. Trim shoe as desired or trim with decorating gel. Use ring-shaped candies for eyelets and licorice for shoelace. Poke holes in toe and along sides for ventilation holes if desired.

THIS CAKE is in top form for your favorite athlete. Tint the accent frosting any color you like to customize the shoe. Decorator gel or shoestring licorice can be used to outline the design. Chewy fruit snack cut into $1/4$-inch-wide strips can be used in place of the licorice for the shoelaces.

TIME-SAVER TIP: Substitute 1 package (1 lb 2.25 oz) yellow cake mix with pudding for the Whole Wheat Applesauce Cake. Prepare and bake as directed on package. Substitute 2 tubs (1 lb each) vanilla ready-to-spread frosting for the Creamy White Frosting

C U T T I N G   A N D   A S S E M B L I N G   A T H L E T I C   S H O E   C A K E

Cut cake lengthwise in half. Cut ends of each half to round.

Place piece 1 on tray; frost top. Place piece 2 on top; round front end for toe. Arrange pieces 3 and 4 to form high-top opening. Trim piece 5 and place in opening for tongue.

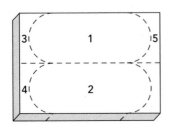

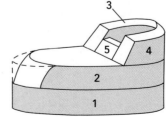

ATHLETIC SHOE CAKE (PAGE 11)

AUTOMOBILE CAKE

NEW CAKE DECORATING

Pound Cake (page 148)

Creamy Vanilla Frosting (page 151)

Desired food color

Tray or cardboard, 13 × 9¹/2 inches, covered

4 cream-filled chocolate sandwich cookies

1 tube (.68 ounce) black or brown decorating gel

Black and yellow licorice beans

1 white and 2 red gum balls

Silver nonpareils

TIME-SAVER TIP: Substitute 1 package (1 lb) pound cake mix for the Pound Cake. Prepare and bake as directed for 2 loaves. Substitute 1¹/2 tubs (1 lb each) vanilla ready-to-spread frosting for the Creamy Vanilla Frosting.

BAKE Pound Cake as directed for 2 loaves. Cut and remove 3 inches from end of 1 loaf. Position pieces as shown in diagram for desired automobile. Freeze cut piece uncovered about 1 hour for easier frosting if desired.

PREPARE Creamy Vanilla Frosting; reserve ¹/2 cup. Tint remaining frosting with food color. Place whole loaf on tray. Frost top with ¹/3 cup colored frosting. Top with cut layer, positioning for desired car. Trim corners for more rounded look if desired. Attach cookies with small amount of frosting for wheels. Draw outline of windows with sharp knife. Frost windows and hubcaps with reserved white frosting. Frost sides and top of car with remaining colored frosting, building up around wheels for fenders.

OUTLINE windows, hood, doors and bumpers with decorating gel. Use licorice beans for grill, door handles and signal lights. Cut gum balls in half; use for headlights and taillights. Make spoke markings on wheel with knife. Press 1 silver nonpareil in center of each wheel. Use silver nonpareils for hood ornament if desired. Remove silver nonpareils before eating.

CUTTING AND ASSEMBLING AUTOMOBILE CAKE

Cut 3 inches from end of one loaf; discard. Leave piece 2 as is for van, or trim 2 inches off one end for sedan or 2 inches diagonally for hatchback.

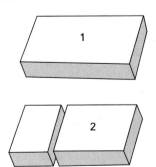

Place piece 1 on tray; frost top. Place piece 2 on top and position for van, sedan or hatchback.

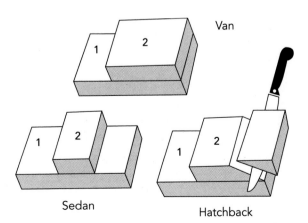

Van

Sedan

Hatchback

PIPE A special message on the slippers to congratulate an aspiring ballerina on her first recital, her birthday or her graduation from dance school. Decorate with plastic ballet dancers or candies as desired.

TIME-SAVER TIP: Substitute 1 package (1 lb 2.25 oz) white cake mix with pudding for the White Cake. Prepare and bake as directed on package. Substitute 2 tubs (1 lb each) vanilla ready-to-spread frosting for the Creamy White Frosting.

White Cake (page 149)
Creamy White Frosting (page 151)
Red food color

Tray or cardboard, 15 × 20 inches, covered
2 yards 1-inch-wide pink ribbon

BAKE White Cake as directed for 13 × 9-inch rectangle. Cut cake as shown in diagram. Freeze cut pieces uncovered about 1 hour for easier frosting if desired. Prepare Creamy White Frosting; reserve 1 cup. Tint remaining frosting with 3 drops food color; reserve 1/2 cup.

ARRANGE cake pieces on tray. Trim pieces to form slippers. Frost sides of both pieces with pink frosting. Frost top of each piece about 3 inches to the edge for the toes, tapering to about 1 inch around the outside edge for the rest of the slipper. Frost the center oval with reserved white frosting. Let frosting set a few minutes. Carefully cover frosting with a paper towel and gently pat to give frosting a fabric-like appearance; remove towel.

PLACE reserved 1/2 cup pink frosting in decorating bag with writing tip #5. Pipe a small beaded border where pink frosting edge meets white edge. Pipe a small bow at each toe. Tie ribbon into bow as desired and attach to the back of the slippers.

CUTTING AND ASSEMBLING BALLET SLIPPERS CAKE

Cut cake lengthwise in half. Trim corners of each half to round.

Arrange cake pieces on tray. Trim pieces to form slippers.

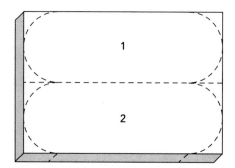

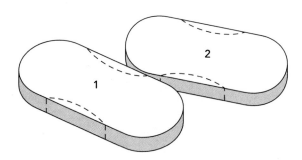

COLORFUL DESIGNS

Feather Design **Dip a piece of unwaxed dental floss or white sewing thread in liquid food color. Stretch it taut and press lines into frosted cake, using new thread for each color. Immediately draw a knife back and forth across line.**

Abstract and Plaid Designs **Dip a piece of unwaxed dental floss or white sewing thread in liquid food color. Stretch it taut and press into frosted cake. Repeat, making desired abstract or plaid design. Use new thread for each color.**

Tic-Tac-Toe Design **Dip a piece of unwaxed dental floss or white sewing thread in liquid food color. Stretch it taut and press into frosted cake to make tic-tac-toe board. Make X's and O's with candy or cereals.**

Yellow Cake (page 150)
Easy Penuche Frosting (page 152)
Tray or cardboard, 15 × 12 inches, covered
1 roll cherry or strawberry chewy fruit snack

30 gummy bear candies
6 ring-shaped hard candies
Chocolate Decorator Frosting (page 150)
2 red cinnamon candies

TIME-SAVER TIP: Substitute 1 package (1 lb 2.25 oz) golden vanilla cake mix with pudding for the Yellow Cake. Prepare as directed on package. Bake as directed in Yellow Cake for muffin cups to make 12 cupcakes and 9-inch square. Substitute 1 tub (1 lb) vanilla ready-to-spread frosting mixed with 7 drops yellow and 1 drop red food color for the Easy Penuche Frosting and $1/2$ tub (1-lb size) chocolate ready-to-spread frosting for the Chocolate Decorator Frosting.

BAKE Yellow Cake as directed for muffin cups to make 12 cupcakes and 9-inch square. Cut cake as shown in diagram. Freeze pieces uncovered about 1 hour for easier frosting if desired. Prepare Easy Penuche Frosting. Arrange pieces on tray to form bus as shown in diagram. Frost cake, attaching pieces with small amount of frosting.

DECORATE bus with strips of fruit snack as shown in photograph. Press gummy bears in windows. Press ring-shaped candies on ends of bus for headlights and taillights.

PREPARE Chocolate Decorator Frosting. Remove paper baking cups from 2 cupcakes; frost sides and tops with chocolate frosting. Cut narrow slice from each chocolate-frosted cupcake; press cupcakes along bottom of bus for wheels. Press 1 ring-shaped candy with cinnamon candy in center on each wheel.

FROST remaining cupcakes with remaining penuche and chocolate frostings. Press 2 gummy bears on each cupcake. Arrange cupcakes around bus.

C U T T I N G   A N D   A S S E M B L I N G   B E A R S - O N - T H E - B U S   C A K E

Cut one $2^{1}/_{2}$-inch wide strip from square cake. Cut $3^{1}/_{2} × 2^{1}/_{2}$-inch rectangle from one end of strip.

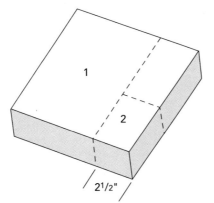

2$^{1}/_{2}$"

Arrange pieces 1 and 2 to form bus.

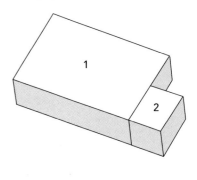

BEARS-ON-THE-BUS CAKE

TIME-SAVER TIP: Substitute 2 packages (1 lb 2.25 oz each) white cake mix with pudding for the Almond Cakes. Prepare and bake as directed on package. Substitute 1 1/2 tubs (1 lb each) vanilla ready-to-spread frosting for the Creamy White Frosting and 1 tub (1-lb size) chocolate ready-to-spread frosting for the Creamy Chocolate Frosting.

2 recipes Almond Cake (page 149)
Creamy White Frosting (page 151)
Tray or cardboard, 18 × 15 inches, covered
Creamy Chocolate Frosting (page 151)

1 roll strawberry chewy fruit snack
2 fudge-striped cookies with choco-late-covered bottoms
Black liquid paste food color

PREPARE 1 recipe Almond Cake as directed for 13 × 9-inch rectangle and 1 recipe as directed for two 8-inch rounds. Cut 13 × 9-inch cake as shown in diagram. Freeze pieces uncovered about 1 hour for easier frosting if desired.

PREPARE Creamy White Frosting. Place cake rounds 3 inches apart on tray for wheels. Prepare Creamy Chocolate Frosting; remove 3/4 cup and reserve. Frost 1-inch-wide strip around edge of each wheel with chocolate frosting; frost centers with white frosting. Arrange 13 × 9-inch piece on tray between wheels. Frost with remaining white frosting. Frost upper left 1 1/2-inch edge with chocolate frosting for seat.

PLACE 1 cookie in center of back wheel for hub and one between wheels for pedal axle. Tint the reserved chocolate frosting with 6 drops food color. Place black frosting in decorator bag with writing tip #3. Pipe spokes and wheel frame on each wheel. Lay strips of fruit snack for bike frame as shown in photograph. Pipe chain and wheel centers with star tip #27. Pipe pedals, handlebars and reflector light holders with writing tip #10. Use small pieces of fruit snack for tips of handlebars and reflector lights.

CUTTING AND ASSEMBLING BICYCLE CAKE

Cut bottom corners of rectangle in arcs to fit round layers. Cut a 3 × 2-inch square in top of cake.

Place cake rounds 3 inches apart on tray; frost. Place piece 1 between wheels.

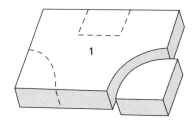

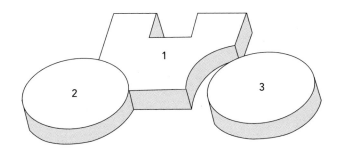

Pound Cake (page 148)
Peanut Butter Frosting (page 151)
2 tablespoons cocoa

1 to 2 tablespoons strawberry preserves
2 teaspoons toasted sesame seed

FOR A little extra fun, sprinkle green-tinted, flaked coconut on top of the jelly (to look like shredded lettuce) before putting on the top layer.

BAKE Pound Cake as directed for 1½-quart casserole. Cut cake horizontally into 3 equal layers. Freeze pieces uncovered about 1 hour for easier frosting if desired. Prepare Peanut Butter Frosting. Place bottom layer on serving plate. Frost side only.

MIX ¾ cup of the remaining frosting and the cocoa; if necessary, stir in 1 to 3 teaspoons milk until spreading consistency. Frost top of bottom layer with part of the cocoa frosting. Place middle (hamburger) layer on top; frost top and side of middle layer with remaining cocoa frosting.

DRIZZLE side of middle layer with preserves to resemble ketchup. Place remaining (rounded) layer on top. Frost with Peanut Butter Frosting. Immediately sprinkle top of cake with sesame seed.

TIME-SAVER TIP: Substitute 1 package (1 lb) pound cake mix for the Pound Cake. Prepare and bake as directed for 1½-quart casserole. Substitute 1 tub (1-lb size) vanilla ready-to-spread frosting mixed with 7 drops yellow and 1 drop red food color for the Peanut Butter Frosting and ½ tub (1-lb size) chocolate ready-to-spread frosting for the frosting mixed with cocoa.

CHOCOLATE FEATHER DESIGN

Drizzle lines with melted chocolate about 1 inch apart across frosted or glazed cake. Immediately draw a knife back and forth across lines to make a "feather" design.

BIG BURGER CAKE

TIME-SAVER TIP: Substitute 1 package (1 lb 2 oz) carrot cake mix or 1 package (1 lb 2.25 oz) yellow cake mix with pudding for the Carrot Cake. Prepare and bake as directed on package. Substitute 1 1/2 tubs (1 lb each) cream cheese ready-to-spread frosting for the Cream Cheese Frosting.

Carrot Cake (page 146)
Cream Cheese Frosting (page 151)
Yellow and red food colors
Tray or cardboard, 18 × 12 inches, covered
1 pink marshmallow-covered chocolate cake ball with creamy filling

1 large gumdrop
Red shoestring licorice
1 roll strawberry chewy fruit snack
3 miniature chocolate chips

BAKE Carrot Cake as directed for 13 × 9-inch rectangle. Cut cake as shown in diagram. Prepare Cream Cheese Frosting; reserve 2 tablespoons. Tint remaining frosting with 2 drops yellow food color. Arrange cake pieces 1 and 2 on tray; frost with 1/3 cup yellow frosting. Place piece 3 on top; frost sides and top.

PUT 4 drops yellow food color in custard cup. Dip back of spoon in color; swirl in sides of cake to make holes. Tint reserved frosting pink with 1 drop red food color. Arrange cake ball and gumdrop on top of cake for mouse; frost gumdrop with pink frosting. Use shoestring licorice for tail and whiskers, fruit snack for ears and chocolate chips for eyes and nose.

CUTTING AND ASSEMBLING CHEESE AND MOUSE CAKE

Cut cake diagonally into 3 pieces.

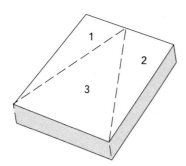

Arrange side pieces on tray; frost top. Place remaining piece on top; frost sides and top.

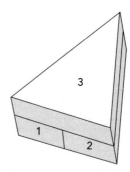

CHEESE AND MOUSE CAKE AND KITTY CAT CAKE (PAGE 24)

FOR A tabby cat, lion or Pekinese puppy, tint the coconut the desired color.

White Cake (page 149)
Creamy White Frosting (page 151)
Tray or cardboard, 14 × 11 inches, covered
1 1/2 cups flaked or shredded coconut

Red shoestring licorice
1 roll strawberry chewy fruit snack
2 blue jelly beans
1 pink jelly bean

TIME-SAVER TIP: Substitute 1 package (1 lb 2.25 oz) white cake mix with pudding for the White Cake. Prepare and bake as directed on package. Substitute 2 tubs (1 lb each) vanilla ready-to-spread frosting for the Creamy White Frosting.

BAKE White Cake as directed for two 8-inch round pans. Cut cakes as shown in diagram. Freeze pieces uncovered about 1 hour for easier frosting if desired. Prepare Creamy White Frosting. Put pieces 1 and 2 together with 1/3 cup frosting. Place cut sides down on tray to form body. Attach remaining pieces with about 1 cup frosting to form kitty as shown in diagram, trimming pieces to fit. Frost cake, shaping cheeks and mouth with small spatula.

SPRINKLE with coconut, pressing gently to adhere. Use shoestring licorice for whiskers. Use jelly beans for nose and eyes. Cut ears and tongue from fruit snack. Use remaining fruit snack to make collar and bow.

CUTTING AND ASSEMBLING KITTY CAT CAKE

Cut one layer in half to form body. Frost top of piece 1; top with piece 2.

Cut second layer to form legs, head, ears and tail.

Place body, cut sides down, on tray. Arrange pieces from second layer around body to form kitty.

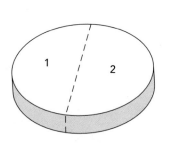

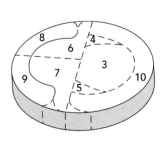

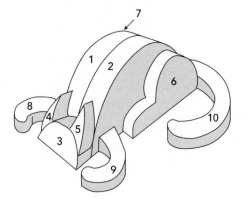

Double Chocolate Cake (page 147)
Tray or cardboard, 18 × 10 inches, covered
White Mountain Frosting
    (page 152)
1 cup flaked or shredded coconut
10 small licorice candies
2 blue licorice candies
1 large black gumdrop, cut in half
1 carrot candy or small piece carrot chewy fruit snack
3 chocolate-covered marshmallow cookies
Black shoestring licorice
1 chocolate-covered butter toffee bar
1 pretzel rod

BAKE Double Chocolate Cake as directed for one 8-inch round and one 9-inch round. Arrange layers on tray to form snowman. Prepare White Mountain Frosting. Frost, attaching pieces with small amount of frosting.

SPRINKLE with coconut, pressing gently to adhere. Use small licorice candies for mouth and buttons, blue licorice candies for eyes, black gumdrop for eyebrows, carrot candy for nose and fruit snack for muffler. Place chocolate-covered cookie on each side of head for earmuffs; attach with shoestring licorice. Cut coffee bar, remaining cookie and pretzel rod in half. Use for legs, shoe and arms.

TIME-SAVER TIP: Substitute 1 package (1 lb. 2.25oz) devil's food cake mix with pudding for the Double Chocolate Cake. Prepare and bake as directed on the package. Substitute 1 package (7.2 ounces) fluffy white frosting mix for the White Mountain Frosting. Prepare as directed on package.

SNOWMAN CAKE

DINOSAUR CAKE

USE MULTICOLORED candy-covered chocolate chips or other candies for scales. Colored decorator frosting in a can or tube can be used in place of the decorating gel.

TIME-SAVER TIP: Substitute 1 package (1 lb 2.25 oz) yellow cake mix with pudding for the Yellow Cake. Prepare and bake as directed on package. Substitute 1½ tubs (1 lb each) vanilla ready-to-spread frosting for the Creamy Vanilla Frosting.

Yellow Cake (page 150)
Creamy Vanilla Frosting (page 151)
Green food color
Tray or cardboard, 18 × 12 inches, covered

1 tube (.68 ounce) black or brown decorating gel
Green candy-coated chocolate chips
Red jelly bean

BAKE Yellow Cake as directed for 13 × 9-inch rectangle. Cut cake as shown in diagram. Freeze pieces uncovered about 1 hour for easier frosting if desired. Prepare Creamy Vanilla Frosting; tint with 6 drops food color. Arrange pieces on tray to form dinosaur as shown in diagram. Frost cake, attaching pieces with small amount of frosting.

LET frosting set a few minutes. Carefully cover with a paper towel and gently pat to give frosting a textured appearance; remove towel. Outline scales, legs, mouth, nose and jelly bean eye with decorating gel. Decorate with candy-coated chocolate chips.

CANDY BUTTERFLIES

For each butterfly, cut a notch on straight sides of two candied fruit slices, slightly below center.

Arrange slices for wings and notches for body as shown. Add shoestring licorice for antenna.

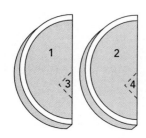

CUTTING AND ASSEMBLING DINOSAUR CAKE

Cut cake to form body, feet and tail of dinosaur.

Arrange pieces to form dinosaur.

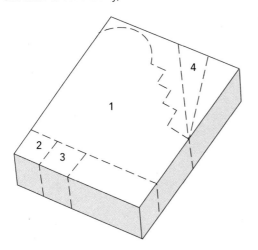

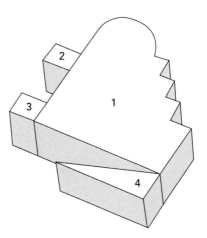

Cherry-Nut Cake (page 149)
Creamy White Frosting (page 151)
Red paste food color
Tray or cardboard, 20 × 12 inches, covered
Assorted colored sugars
1 red licorice twist

Small silver nonpareils
2 red gumdrops
4 small red round jelly candies
4 capsule-shaped red candies
1 roll strawberry chewy fruit snack

TIME-SAVER TIP: Substitute 1 package (1 lb 2.25 oz) yellow cake mix with pudding for the Cherry-Nut Cake. Prepare and bake as directed on package. Substitute 2 tubs (1 lb each) vanilla ready-to-spread frosting for the Creamy White Frosting.

PREPARE Cherry-Nut Cake as directed for 13 × 9-inch rectangle. Cut cake as shown in diagram. Freeze cut pieces uncovered about 1 hour for easier frosting if desired. Prepare Creamy White Frosting; reserve $1/3$ of frosting. Tint remaining frosting with 10 drops food color. Tint $1/2$ cup red frosting with 2 additional drops food color.

ARRANGE cake pieces on tray to form guitar as shown in diagram. Frost top and side of neck and sounding board with white frosting, reserving $1/4$ cup frosting. Frost the rest of the cake with the lighter red frosting. Sprinkle sounding board with colored sugars. Place deeper red frosting in decorating bag with writing tip #4. Pipe frets on neck. Pipe beaded border around sounding board where the red and white frostings meet.

PIPE 2 rows of stars, 3 inches long, for bridge with the $1/4$ cup reserved white frosting and star tip #18. Cut licorice twists into 3-inch lengths; place on sounding board as shown. Place silver nonpareils next to licorice twists and on neck between frets as shown. Add gumdrops for control knobs, small candies for string pegs and the capsule-shaped candies at the top side edge for tuning pegs. Cut 4 pieces of fruit snack $1/8$ inch wide by 18 inches long with a knife and a straight edge. Place the strings on the cake, tucking ends into the bridge and wrapping other ends around the top and side pegs. Cut strings $1/4$ inch from each tuning peg, tucking the tails into the frosting. Remove silver nonpareils before eating.

ELECTRIC GUITAR CAKE

CUTTING AND ASSEMBLING ELECTRIC GUITAR CAKE

Cut cake to form body and neck of guitar.

Arrange pieces to form guitar.

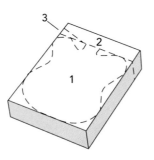

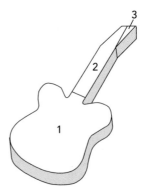

Lemon–Poppy Seed Cake (page 150)

Tray or cardboard, 18 × 13 inches, covered

Creamy Citrus Frosting (page 151)

Blue, green and yellow food colors

Yellow sugar

Pink Sugar

1 yellow and black round licorice candy

ANGLERS AND tropical fish lovers will be hooked on this cake! For a fun presentation, cover the board with blue plastic wrap and decorate with green decorating gel or frosting for seaweed. Add sea creatures and shells as desired.

BAKE Lemon–Poppy Seed Cake as directed for 13 × 9-inch rectangle. Cut cake as shown in diagram. Freeze pieces uncovered about 1 hour for easier frosting if desired. Arrange pieces on tray to form fish as shown in diagram. Prepare Creamy Citrus Frosting. Frost cake, attaching pieces with small amount of frosting.

DROP 4 drops blue food color along top of fish, 4 drops green along center and 4 drops yellow along bottom. Starting from top edge of fish, blend colors into frosting, working blue down into green and green down into yellow. Use back of spoon to form scales. Define lips with edge of spatula. Mark tail and fins with fork. Sprinkle bottom half of fish with yellow sugar and top half with pink sugar. Use licorice candy for eye.

TIME-SAVER TIP: Substitute 1 package (1 lb 2.25 oz) yellow cake mix with pudding for the Lemon–Poppy Seed Cake. Prepare and bake as directed on package. Substitute 1 tub (1-lb size) vanilla ready-to-spread frosting for the Creamy Citrus Frosting.

CHOCOLATE FLOWER DESIGN

Drizzle round frosted or glazed cake with melted chocolate, beginning with small circle in center and encircling with larger circle, $1/2$ inch outside the other. Immediately draw a knife from outside edge inward and from center outward alternately 4 to 8 times to make flower design.

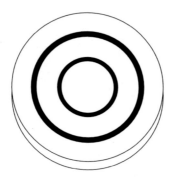 

FISH CAKE

CUTTING AND ASSEMBLING FISH CAKE

Cut cake to form body, fins and mouth of fish.

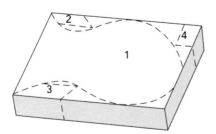

Arrange pieces to form fish.

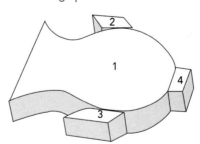

DIP THE tops of the cupcakes in colored sugars, if you like, instead of coloring them with food color. Jumbo gum balls or other round candies can be used if you don't have a small cupcake pan.

TIME-SAVER TIP: Substitute 1 package (1 lb 2.25 oz) yellow cake mix with pudding for the Almond Cake. Prepare and bake as directed for Almond Cake assorted pans. Substitute 1½ tubs (1 lb each) vanilla ready-to-spread frosting for the Creamy Almond Frosting.

Almond Cake (page 149)
Creamy Almond Frosting
(page 151)
Blue, green, red and yellow food colors

Tray or cardboard, 17 × 12 inches, covered
1 tube (.68 ounce) red decorating gel

BAKE Almond Cake as directed for small muffin cups to make 12 small cupcakes, 8-inch round and 8-inch square. Cut cakes as shown in diagram. Freeze pieces uncovered about 1 hour for easier frosting if desired. Prepare Creamy Almond Frosting.

FROST each cupcake with scant tablespoon frosting. Place 1 drop blue food color in center of each of 3 cupcakes. Spread color through frosting. Repeat with green, red and yellow food colors and remaining cupcakes. Arrange cake pieces on tray to form gum ball machine as shown in diagram. Frost piece 1 with ⅔ cup frosting. Place cupcakes on top.

TINT remaining frosting with 7 drops yellow food color. Frost remaining pieces, attaching them with small amount of frosting. Outline workings of machine as desired with red gel.

CUTTING AND ASSEMBLING GUM BALL MACHINE CAKE

Cut small piece from each side of round cake.

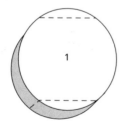

Cut a 1-inch-wide strip down each side of square cake, to within 1 inch of bottom. Cut a 4-inch piece from each strip.

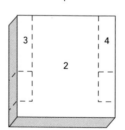

Arrange pieces to form gum ball base and globe

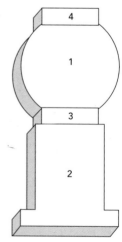

GUM BALL MACHINE CAKE

Marble Cake (page 149)
Creamy Chocolate Frosting
(page 151)
Tray or cardboard, 14 × 10 inches,
covered

2 large black gumdrops
1/3 cup powdered sugar
1 teaspoon milk
1 teaspoon margarine or butter,
softened

TIME-SAVER TIP: Substitute
1 package (1 lb 2.25 oz) marble
cake mix with pudding for the
Marble Cake. Prepare and bake as
directed on package. Substitute
1 tub (1-lb size) chocolate ready-
to-spread frosting for the Creamy
Chocolate Frosting.

BAKE Marble Cake as directed for two 9-inch rounds. Reserve
1 layer for another use. Cut cake as shown in diagram. Freeze pieces
uncovered about 1 hour for easier frosting if desired. Prepare
Creamy Chocolate Frosting. Arrange cake pieces on tray to form
horse's head as shown in diagram; trim pieces 2 and 3 to form ears.

FROST cake, attaching pieces with small amount of frosting. Place
gumdrops on face for eyes. Use fork to draw hair into frosting,
bringing frosting up over gumdrops to form eyelids. Mark nose
indentations with small spatula. Mix powdered sugar, milk and
margarine. Spread on face between ears and eyes with fork to form
forelock.

CUTTING AND ASSEMBLING HORSE'S HEAD CAKE

Cut cake to form horse's face and ears.

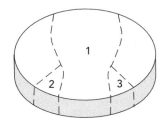

Arrange pieces to form horse's head.

CUTTING AND ASSEMBLING MONKEY CAKE (PAGE 36)

Cut cake to form body and arms.

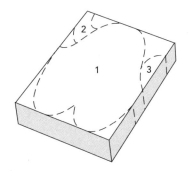

Arrange pieces to form monkey.

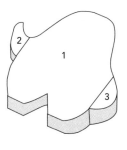

MONKEY CAKE (PAGE 36) AND HORSE'S HEAD CAKE

MONKEY CAKE

Dark Cocoa Cake (page 147)
Creamy Cocoa Frosting (page 151)

1/2 cup powdered sugar
2 teaspoons milk
Tray or cardboard, 16 × 14 inches, covered
Miniature chocolate chips
2 banana chips
1 pecan half
1 banana-shaped candy

BAKE Dark Cocoa Cake as directed for 13 × 9-inch rectangle. Cut cake as shown in diagram (on page 35). Freeze pieces uncovered about 1 hour for easier frosting if desired. Prepare Creamy Cocoa Frosting. Mix 1 tablespoon frosting, the powdered sugar and milk; reserve.

ARRANGE pieces on tray to form monkey as shown in diagram; trim pieces 2 and 3 to fit for arms. Draw outline of face with sharp knife (see photo on page 34). Frost sides and top of cake, except face, with cocoa frosting, attaching pieces with small amount of frosting. Make lines in frosting with tines of fork to resemble fur. Fill in face with reserved frosting, reserving 2 tablespoons. Place reserved frosting in decorating bag with writing tip #4. Pipe outlines of hands and face. Use chocolate chips for eyebrows, banana chips for eyes, pecan half for nose and banana candy for mouth. Place banana-shaped cookie in monkey's hand if desired.

TIME-SAVER TIP: Substitute 1 package (1 lb 2.25 oz) devil's food cake mix with pudding for the Dark Cocoa Cake. Prepare and bake as directed on package. Substitute 1 1/2 tubs (1 lb each) chocolate ready-to-spread frosting for the Creamy Cocoa Frosting.

IN-LINE SKATE CAKE

IF YOU want to make a cake for an ice-skating party, just eliminate the wheels and brake.

Almond Cake (page 149)
Creamy Almond Frosting (page 151)
Green and yellow food colors
Tray or cardboard, 18 × 15 inches, covered
1 roll strawberry chewy fruit snack
4 fudge-striped cookies with chocolate-covered bottoms
1 tube (.68 ounce) brown or black decorating gel
8 ring-shaped hard candies

BAKE Almond Cake as directed for 13 × 9-inch rectangle. Cut cake as shown in diagram. Freeze pieces uncovered about 1 hour for easier frosting if desired. Prepare Creamy Almond Frosting. Tint 1/3 cup frosting with 3 drops green food color. Arrange pieces on tray to form skate as shown in diagram, trimming pieces to fit. Frost cake with white frosting, attaching pieces with frosting.

OUTLINE inner throat and tongue of skate with toothpick. Tint 2 tablespoons white frosting with 2 drops yellow food color; frost inner throat. Frost tongue and back of throat with green frosting. Use fruit snack to form brake, strap and back of throat. Make 4 slits in bottom edge of blade and insert cookies for wheels. Outline skate and blade with decorating gel. Use ring candies for eyelets and wheel axles. Cut 1/4-inch wide strips of fruit snack and use for laces.

TIME-SAVER TIP: Substitute 1 package (1 lb 2.25 oz) white cake mix with pudding for the Almond Cake. Prepare and bake as directed on package. Substitute 1 1/2 tubs (1 lb each) vanilla ready-to-spread frosting for the Creamy Almond Frosting.

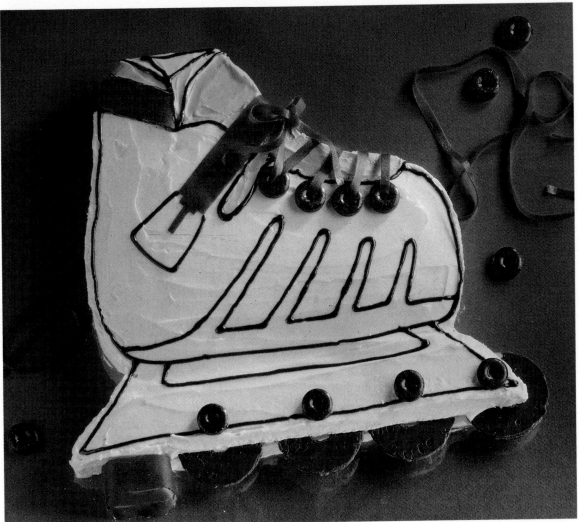

CUTTING AND ASSEMBLING IN-LINE SKATE CAKE

Cut a 2-inch-wide strip from one end of cake; trim end at a diagonal for back end of wheel case. Cut remaining piece of cake to form boot, front end of wheel case and brake stop.

Arrange pieces to form in-line skate.

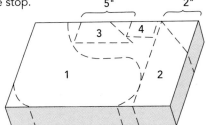

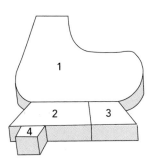

CUT-OUT AND SHAPED CAKES

PANDA CAKE

TIME-SAVER TIP: Substitute
1 package (1 lb 2.25 oz) fudge
marble or devil's food cake mix
with pudding for the Marble Cake.
Prepare and bake as directed on
package. Substitute 1 package
(7.2 ounces) fluffy white frosting
mix for the White Mountain
Frosting. Prepare as directed on
package.

Marble Cake (page 149)
Tray or cardboard, 16 × 10 inches, covered
White Mountain Frosting (page 152)
$^1/_2$ cup flaked coconut
8 chocolate wafers, about 2 inches in diameter

1 large marshmallow
2 chocolate-covered candies
1 small black or red gumdrop
Black shoestring licorice
$^1/_3$ cup flaked coconut
1 teaspoon cocoa

BAKE Marble Cake as directed for one 8-inch round and one 9-inch round. Cut 9-inch round as shown in diagram. Arrange pieces on tray to form panda as shown in diagram.

PREPARE White Mountain Frosting. Frost cake, attaching pieces with small amount of frosting. Sprinkle body with $^1/_2$ cup flaked coconut, pressing gently to adhere. Press 2 wafers into top of heat at 45° angle for ears. Place 2 wafers for background of eyes and 4 on body for paws, placing bottom 2 wafers at 45° angle on bottom edge of cake.

CUT marshmallow crosswise in half; place each half on a chocolate wafer for eyes. Place chocolate candies on marshmallow halves for pupils; fasten with small dab of frosting if necessary. Use small gumdrop for nose and shoestring licorice for mouth and outline of legs. Toss $^1/_3$ cup coconut and the cocoa; carefully sprinkle within outlines of legs and on bottom portion of body.

CUTTING AND ASSEMBLING PANDA CAKE

Cut small curved piece from one side of 9-inch layer.

Join 8-inch layer to cut section of cake 1.

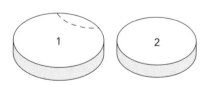
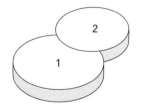

THIS CAKE will feed the whole team! The Baseball Caps can be eliminated if you just want a ball. For a basketball, tint the frosting orange and use licorice laces for a basketball design. For a soccer ball, outline the design with a toothpick and fill in every other section with desired colored frostings.

TIME-SAVER TIP: Substitute 2 packages (1 lb 2.25 oz) yellow cake mix with pudding for the Yellow Cake. Bake as directed in Yellow Cake recipe for 2-quart round casserole. Substitute 1 package (1 lb 2.25 oz) devil's food cake mix with pudding for the Double Chocolate Cake. Prepare and bake as directed on package for cupcakes. Substitute 5 tubs (1 lb each) vanilla ready-to-spread frosting for the Creamy White Frosting.

2 recipes Yellow Cake (page 150)
Creamy White Frosting (page 151)
Tray or cardboard, 15 inches round, covered
Red shoestring licorice
Baseball Caps (below)
Decorating gel, if desired

BAKE 1 recipe Yellow Cake as directed for 2-quart round casserole. Repeat with second recipe. Prepare Creamy White Frosting. Place 1 cake, rounded side up, on tray. Trim top to make a flat surface. Spread with $1/3$ cup frosting. Trim top of second layer flat. Place upside down on top of first layer to make a ball. Frost entire cake. Use red licorice for seams on baseball as shown. Pipe desired message with decorating gel.

BASEBALL CAPS

Double Chocolate Cake (page 147)
Creamy White Frosting (page 151)
Assorted food colors
Black shoestring licorice
Candy-coated fruit pieces
Assorted candied fruit slices
Decorating gel, if desired

BAKE Double Chocolate Cake as directed for muffin cups to make cupcakes. Prepare Creamy White Frosting. Divide frosting among small bowls for as many colors as desired. Stir 2 drops desired food color into frosting in each bowl. Trim top of each cupcake to make a flat surface. Frost bottoms and sides of cupcakes with assorted colored frostings. Place as many cupcakes around baseball as will fit. Place remaining cupcakes on separate tray. Starting at center top of each cap, place pieces of black shoestring licorice down sides for seams. Place 1 candy-coated fruit piece at center top. Use fruit slices for brims (trim fruit slices if necessary). Pipe child's name or team initial on caps if desired.

PATCHWORK DESIGN

Mark servings in the frosting of a square or rectangular cake with a knife or toothpick. Fill the squares with chopped nuts, miniature candy-coated chocolate chips or pieces, confetti candy bits, crushed candies, colored sugars, fruit-shaped candies, tinted coconut, chopped dried fruits, chocolate-dipped fruits, small shaped cookies or crackers or cereals to look like a patchwork quilt.

Buttermilk Spice Cake (page 146)
White Mountain Frosting (page 152)
Tray or cardboard, 20 × 18 inches, covered

1 tablespoon cocoa
14 × 4-inch piece of aluminum foil*
5 ring-shaped hard candies

BAKE Buttermilk Spice Cake as directed for 13 × 9-inch rectangle. Cut cake as shown in diagram. Freeze pieces uncovered about 1 hour for easier frosting if desired. Prepare White Mountain Frosting; reserve 1 cup. Arrange pieces on tray to form sailboat as shown in diagram, leaving space between sails for mast. Frost sails with remaining frosting.

GENTLY fold cocoa into frosting until blended. Frost hull of sailboat with cocoa frosting. Roll up aluminum foil for mast; place between sails. Use ring-shaped candies for portholes.

TIME-SAVER TIP: Substitute 1 package (1 lb 2.25 oz) spice, devil's food or yellow cake mix with pudding for the Buttermilk Spice Cake. Prepare and bake as directed on package. Substitute 1 package (7.2 ounces) fluffy white frosting mix for the White Mountain Frosting. Prepare as directed on package.

C U T T I N G   A N D   A S S E M B L I N G   S A I L B O A T   C A K E

Cut cake diagonally into 3 pieces.

Arrange pieces to form sailboat, leaving space between sails for mast.

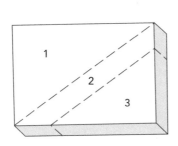

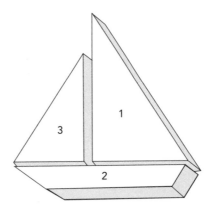

SAILBOAT CAKE

*A 14 × 4-inch piece of wrapping or shelf paper can be substituted for aluminum foil; secure with tape.

SPACESHIP CAKE

Yellow Cake (page 150)
Creamy Vanilla Frosting (page 151)
Tray or cardboard, 17 × 12 inches, covered

1 roll strawberry chewy fruit snack
1 tube (.68 ounce) black decorating gel

TIME-SAVER TIP: Substitute 1 package (1 lb 2.25 oz) yellow cake mix with pudding for the Yellow Cake. Prepare and bake as directed on package. Substitute 1½ tubs (1 lb) each vanilla ready-to-spread frosting for the Creamy Vanilla Frosting.

BAKE Yellow Cake as directed for 13 × 9-inch rectangle. Cut cake as shown in diagram. Freeze pieces uncovered about 1 hour for easier frosting if desired. Prepare Creamy Vanilla Frosting.

PLACE cake piece 1 on tray. Frost with about 1¼ cups frosting. Arrange pieces 2, 3 and 4 as shown in diagram, trimming to fit, standing up piece 3 for top fin. Trim point of piece 2 for nose of ship. Frost cake with remaining frosting. Let frosting set a few minutes. Carefully cover with a paper towel and gently pat to give a fabric-like appearance; remove towel. Use fruit snack for strips as shown in photograph. Outline as desired with decorating gel.

CUTTING AND ASSEMBLING SPACESHIP CAKE

Cut cake to form body pieces of spaceship.

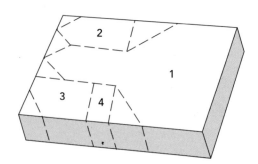

Place piece 1 on tray; frost. Arrange remaining pieces to form spaceship, standing up piece 3 for top fin.

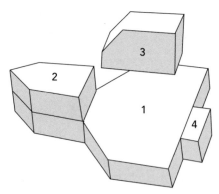

SPACESHIP CAKE

YOU CAN use a lollipop, candy cane or other candy instead of the ice cream cone, or you can eliminate it altogether.

TIME-SAVER TIP: Substitute 1 package (1 lb 2.25 oz) devil's food cake mix with pudding for the Double Chocolate Cake. Prepare and bake as directed on package—except decrease water to 1 cup and stir 1 cup miniature chocolate chips into batter. Substitute 1 tub (1-lb size) chocolate ready-to-spread frosting for the Creamy Chocolate Frosting.

Double Chocolate Cake (page 147)
Creamy Chocolate Frosting (page 151)
Tray or cardboard, 17 × 12 inches, covered
1 roll strawberry chewy fruit snack
2 large black gumdrops
2 large red gumdrops
Red shoestring licorice
Pink nonpareil candies
6 medium red gumdrops, cut in half
¹/₂ ice cream cone

BAKE Double Chocolate Cake as directed for one 8-inch round and one 9-inch square. Cut cake as shown in diagram. Freeze pieces uncovered about 1 hour for easier frosting if desired. Prepare Creamy Chocolate Frosting. Arrange pieces on tray to form a teddy bear as shown in diagram. Frost cake, attaching pieces with small amount of frosting, reserving 2 tablespoons frosting.

MAKE fur marks in frosting with fork, leaving face smooth. Cut tongue, ears and bow from fruit snack. Use black gumdrops for eyes, large red gumdrop for nose and licorice for mouth. Accent bow with other large red gumdrop. Sprinkle nonpareils on cheeks and paws. Use 3 medium gumdrop halves for pads on each paw. Position ice cream cone, cut side down, between top paws for honey pot. Place reserved frosting in decorating bag with writing tip #3. Pipe *honey* on cone.

CUTTING AND ASSEMBLING TEDDY BEAR CAKE

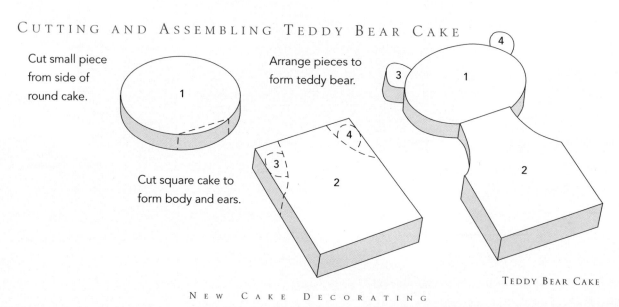

Cut small piece from side of round cake.

Cut square cake to form body and ears.

Arrange pieces to form teddy bear.

TEDDY BEAR CAKE

Double Chocolate Cake
    (page 147)

Creamy Chocolate Frosting
    (page 151)

Tray or cardboard, 25 ×
    13 inches, covered

4 black-and-white striped
    licorice candies

8 pink-and-black round licorice
    candies

Black shoestring licorice

4 cream-filled chocolate cookies

1 round pink licorice candy

1 black cylinder-shaped licorice
    candy

2 pieces popcorn

1 solid chocolate drop in foil
    wrapping

3 teddy bear-shaped cookies

5 sticks red licorice twists

Semisweet rainbow morsels

Creamy Vanilla Frosting
    (page 151)

10 candy sticks (3 inches)

Animal-shaped cookies or
    crackers

6 yellow-and-black round
    licorice candies

Fruit-shaped candies

Yellow and red food colors

4 yellow square licorice candies

1 round blue licorice candy

TIME-SAVER TIP: Substitute 1
package (1 lb 2.25 oz) chocolate
fudge cake mix with pudding for
the Double Chocolate Cake.
Prepare as directed on package
except bake as directed in Double
Chocolate Cake recipe for 9-inch
loaves. Substitute 1 tub (1-lb size)
chocolate ready-to-spread frosting
for the Creamy Chocolate Frosting
and 1 tub (1-lb size) vanilla ready-
to-spread frosting for the Creamy
Vanilla Frosting.

BAKE Double Chocolate Cake as directed for two 9-inch loaves. Cut cake as shown in diagram (right), being careful not to cut all the way through piece 1 when removing piece 2. Trim pieces 3 and 6 flat on top. Freeze pieces uncovered about 1 hour for easier frosting. Prepare Creamy Chocolate Frosting.

PLACE piece 1 on tray for engine, stacking piece 2 on top for engine house, as shown in diagram. Frost with chocolate frosting. Cut each black-and-white striped licorice candy into thirds. Place on front of engine, slanting outward to simulate a cow catcher. Cut 6 pink-and-black round licorice candies in half; use for wheels. Connect front wheels with small pieces of shoestring licorice. Attach cookies on engine with small amount of frosting to simulate a boiler. Place pink licorice candy on front of boiler for headlight. Attach black cylinder-shaped licorice candy to boiler for smoke-stack. Attach popcorn with frosting to smokestack for smoke. Use unwrapped chocolate drop for bell and teddy bear-shaped cookies for engineers. Outline top edges, on back of engine, with licorice twists to form coal car. Fill with semisweet rainbow morsels.

PREPARE Creamy Vanilla Frosting. Place piece 3 on tray for log car. Frost with 1/2 cup vanilla frosting. Stack candy sticks to simulate logs. Cut 2 yellow-and-black licorice candies in half for wheels.

PLACE piece 4 on tray for animal car. Trim top round if desired. Tint 1/2 cup vanilla frosting with 6 drops yellow food color; frost car. Place animal-shaped cookies on top of car and in window outlined with shoestring licorice. Cut 2 pink-and-black licorice candies in half for wheels.

PLACE piece 6 on tray for fruit car. Frost with 1/2 cup vanilla frosting. Fill with fruit-shaped candies. Cut 2 yellow-and-black licorice candies in half for wheels.

PLACE piece 5 on tray for caboose. Trim to make shorter and rounded on top if desired. Tint 1/2 cup vanilla frosting with 2 drops red food color. Frost car, forming a mound of frosting on top of caboose. Cut 2 yellow-and-black licorice candies in half for wheels. Use shoestring licorice to outline railing and door on caboose. Use yellow square licorice candy for windows and door handle. Place blue licorice candy and teddy bear-shaped cookie on top. Connect cars together with pieces of licorice twists.

CUTTING AND ASSEMBLING TRAIN CAKE

Cut narrow strip lengthwise from each side of one loaf. Remove a 1½-inch-wide, 1½-inch-thick section from piece 1, being careful not to cut all the way through.

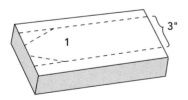

Place piece 2 on top of piece 1 for engine house.

Cut second loaf crosswise into fourths.

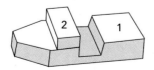

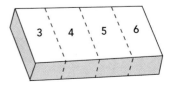

TWO

Festive Holiday Cakes

Holiday Pinecone Cake *52*

Christmas Tree Cake *53*

Mini Bûche de Noël Cakes *55*

Holiday Quilt Cake *56*

Peppermint Cream Cake *57*

Gingerbread Cake Cottage *58*

Let's Celebrate Cake *60*

Chocolate Heart Cake *61*

Cake Full of Hearts *63*

Easter Bunny Cake *64*

Easter Cross Cake *66*

Pot-o'-Gold Cake *68*

Firecracker Cakes *70*

Jack-o'-Lantern Cake *71*

Black Cat Cake *73*

Spiderweb Cake *74*

Turkey Gobbler Cake *76*

Thanksgiving Cake *78*

Fall Angel Food Cake *79*

Hanukkah Dreidel Cake *80*

Holiday Pinecone Cake (page 52)

CARROT CAKE (page 146) and two recipes of Cream Cheese Frosting (page 151) can also be used to make this stunning holiday cake.

TIME-SAVER TIP: Substitute 1 package (1 lb 2.25 oz) yellow cake mix with pudding for the Pumpkin-Gingerbread Cake. Prepare and bake as directed on package.

2 cups powdered sugar
2 tablespoons meringue powder
$^1/_4$ cup water
Green food color
Pumpkin-Gingerbread Cake (page 148)
Creamy White Frosting (page 151)

2 tablespoons cocoa
6 horn-shaped corn snacks
Tray or cardboard, 16 × 12 inches, covered
1 tube (.68 ounce) red decorating gel

DRAW a pair of lines, $1^1/_2$ inches apart, down the length of a page of ruled paper. Make 2 more pairs. Place under sheet of waxed paper. Beat powdered sugar, meringue powder and water with standard mixer on medium speed or with hand mixer on high speed about 2 minutes or until stiff peaks form. Tint with 3 drops green food color. (Stir in $^1/_2$ teaspoon cocoa if desired for a dull green color.) Place in decorating bag with writing tip #5. Pipe 140 pine needles, $1^1/_2$ inches long, inside each pair of lines using the rules as a guide. Allow to dry at least 8 hours. Bake Pumpkin-Gingerbread Cake as directed for 13 × 9-inch rectangle. Prepare Creamy White Frosting. Mix cocoa and 1 cup frosting. Place a corn snack on waxed paper. Starting at pointed end, pipe three petals in a circular motion with cocoa frosting and petal tip #104. Continue making petals, 1 row at a time, alternating and adding loops to shape pinecone. Finish with the bottom row, completely covering open end of corn snack. Repeat with the 5 other corn snacks. Allow to dry several hours.

PLACE cake on tray. Reserve $1^3/_4$ cups frosting. Frost top of cake with remaining white frosting. Place $1^1/_4$ cups of the reserved frosting in decorating bag. Pipe a shell border around base of cake with star tip #5. Pipe a double shell border around top edge of cake with star tip #18.

CAREFULLY remove pinecones from waxed paper and arrange on cake in upper left and lower right corners. Pipe pine branches with remaining cocoa frosting with writing tip #5. Tint remaining $^1/_2$ cup frosting with 3 drops green food color. Pipe holly leaves with leaf tip #67. Pipe desired message on cake with red decorating gel. Pipe red dots for holly berries on holly leaves. Carefully remove pine needles from waxed paper and insert them around pinecones and along branches.

White Cake (page 149)
White Mountain Frosting (page 152)
Green food color
Tray or cardboard, 15 × 13 inches, covered

1 chocolate coated butter toffee bar
1 tube (.68 ounce) green decorating gel
1 large yellow gumdrop
Nonpareil mint chips

TIME-SAVER TIP: Substitute 1 package (1 lb 2.25 oz) white cake mix with pudding for the White Cake. Prepare and bake as directed on package. Substitute 1 package (7.2 ounces) fluffy white frosting mix for the White Mountain Frosting. Prepare as directed on package.

BAKE White Cake as directed for 13 × 9-inch rectangle. Cut cake as shown in diagram. Freeze pieces uncovered about 1 hour for easier frosting if desired. Prepare White Mountain Frosting.

ARRANGE cake pieces 1 and 2 on tray; frost top. Place piece 3 on top; frost sides and top. Dip fork into food color and draw through frosting to create boughs. Insert toffee bar into end of tree to make trunk. Draw light strings with decorating gel. Roll yellow gumdrop on heavily sugared surface into circle 1/8 inch thick; cut into star and place at top of tree. Place nonpareil mint chips on strings for lights.

CUTTING AND ASSEMBLING CHRISTMAS TREE CAKE

Cut cake diagonally into three pieces.

Arrange side pieces on tray; frost top. Place remaining piece on top; frost sides and top.

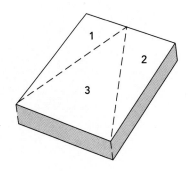

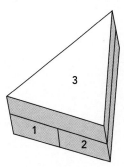

White Cake (page 149)
Creamy Chocolate Frosting
   (page 151)

12 Gumdrop Holly (below)

THESE MINI logs are simple enough for children to make. For a more elegant look, decorate the finished cakes with Chocolate Twigs (page 144) and Chocolate Leaves (page 78) and dust with cocoa. They can also be decorated with gumdrop hatchets for President's Day (page 70).

BAKE White Cake as directed for 24 cupcakes. Prepare Creamy Chocolate Frosting. Put 2 cupcakes together end-to-end with small amount frosting to make logs. Frost sides, leaving ends unfrosted. Make strokes in frosting with fork to resemble bark. Arrange 1 Gumdrop Holly on each log.

TIME-SAVER TIP: Substitute 1 package (1 lb 2.25 oz) white cake mix with pudding for the White Cake. Prepare and bake as directed on package for cupcakes. Substitute 1½ tubs (1 lb each) chocolate ready-to-spread frosting for the Creamy Chocolate Frosting.

Christmas Designs

Gumdrop Holly **For each holly, roll 2 or 3 large green gumdrops, one at a time, on heavily sugared surface until ⅛ inch thick. Cut to resemble holly leaves. Arrange leaves close together; add 3 red cinnamon candies for holly berries.**

Holiday Jelly Bells **Tint 2 tablespoons orange marmalade with 2 drops green food color, and 1 tablespoon orange marmalade with 3 drops red food color. Mark 3 bells, using bell-shaped cookie cutter, on top of cake frosted with white frosting. Fill 2 bells with green marmalade and 1 bell with red marmalade. Dip toothpick into additional green food color and draw lines to connect bells.**

CHRISTMAS TREE CAKE (PAGE 53) AND MINI BÛCHE DE NOËL CAKES

THIS QUILT design is lovely for any occasion: Use pastel colors for showers and bright colors for birthdays.

Chocolate-Cherry Cake (page 147)
Tray or cardboard, 16 × 12 inches, covered
Creamy Vanilla Frosting (page 151)
1 tube (4.25 ounces) green decorating icing
1 tube (4.25 ounces) red decorating icing
Assorted candies and colored
*   sugars*

BAKE Chocolate-Cherry Cake as directed for 13 × 9-inch rectangle. Place cake on tray. Prepare Creamy Vanilla Frosting; remove 1 cup and reserve. Frost cake with remaining frosting.

PIPE lines with green or red icing to divide cake into 24 squares. Decorate every other square with green and red icing, candies or sugars as desired to resemble quilt pattern. Place reserved frosting in decorating bag with star tip #18. Pipe border around top and bottom edges of cake.

TIME-SAVER TIP: Substitute 1 package (1 lb 2.25 oz) devil's food cake mix with pudding for the Chocolate-Cherry Cake. Prepare and bake as directed on package—except fold 1/2 cup chopped maraschino cherries, well drained, into batter. Substitute 1 1/2 tubs (1 lb each) sour cream or vanilla ready-to-spread frosting for the Creamy Vanilla Frosting.

HOLIDAY QUILT CAKE AND PEPPERMINT CREAM
CAKE (PAGE 57)

PEPPERMINT CREAM CAKE

Angel Food Cake (page 145)
3 cups whipping (heavy cream)
1 1/2 cup powdered sugar
1 teaspoon peppermint extract

Red food color
2 small candy cones or 3 table-
spoons crushed peppermint
candy

BAKE Angel Food Cake as directed. Remove cake from pan; place upside down. Slice off top of cake about 1 inch down and reserve. Cut down into cake 1 inch from outer edge and 1 inch from edge of hole, leaving substantial walls on each side. Remove center with a spoon or curved knife, being careful to leave a base of cake 1 inch thick.

BEAT whipping cream, powdered sugar, peppermint extract and 12 drops food color in chilled bowl until stiff. Spoon two-thirds of the whipped cream into cake cavity. Press mixture firmly into cavity.

REPLACE top of cake and press gently. Frost cake with remaining whipped cream. Refrigerate at least 4 hours. Just before serving, arrange candy canes on top or sprinkle with crushed candy. Garnish with fresh mint if desired. Refrigerate any remaining cake.

TIME-SAVER TIP: Substitute 1 package (1 lb) white angel food cake mix for the Angel Food Cake. Prepare and bake as directed on package.

CUTTING AND FILLING PEPPERMINT CREAM CAKE

Slice off top of cake about 1 inch down.

Cut into cake 1 inch from edge and 1 inch from hole. Spoon half of the whipped cream into cavity of cake

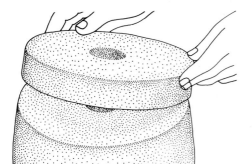
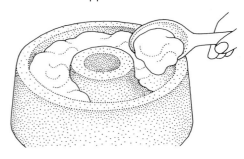

GINGERBREAD CAKE COTTAGE

THIS ADORABLE cottage can be made out of any flavor 13 × 9-inch rectangle cake. Use it as a housewarming gift, and decorate it to match the new house!

Pumpkin-Gingerbread Cake
(page 148)

2 recipes Easy Penuche Frosting
(page 152)

Creamy Vanilla Frosting
(page 151)

Tray or cardboard, 12 × 9 inches, covered

3 multi-colored striped candy sticks (5 inches each)

3 or 4 chocolate sugar wafer cookies (4¹/₂-inch length)

2 green licorice beans

4 vanilla sugar wafer cookies (4¹/₂-inch length)

PREPARE and bake Pumpkin-Gingerbread Cake as directed. Cut cake as shown in diagram. Prepare Easy Penuche Frosting, remove 1¹/₂ cups. Cover remaining frosting and reserve. Place piece 1 on tray; frost top. Frost top of piece 2; top with piece 3. Stand pieces 2 and 3 upright on piece 1. Trim corners and base so pieces fit smoothly. (Roof point will be slightly off center.) Place cake in freezer; freeze about 1 hour or until firm.

PREPARE Creamy Vanilla Frosting. Remove cake from freezer. Frost exterior of house with reserved penuche frosting. Smooth frosting on front, sides and back of house with slightly dampened large spatula. Use the edge of a small spatula to press lines on front of cottage to simulate logs.

PLACE about ¹/₃ cup vanilla frosting at a time in decorating bag with writing tip #6. Break one striped candy stick in half. Pipe a strip of frosting down the length of each candy stick half. Press one half to each vertical front edge of house. Attach remaining candy sticks along front roof lines. Let set about 30 minutes.

CUT chocolate wafer cookies to make doors and shutters. Attach with small amount of frosting piped to the back of each piece. Pipe outlines of window panes and frames. Attach licorice beans for door handles. Trim shutters with decorative sprinkles if desired

CUT vanilla sugar wafer cookies to make chimney pieces. The back piece should be 1¹/₂ inches in length, the front piece 2¹/₂ inches in length. For the sides, cut two pieces each 2 inches in length. Cut one end of each piece at an angle, so that the side facing the back measures 1¹/₂ inches in length and the side facing the front measures 2¹/₂ inches in length. Pipe frosting on inside vertical edges of two slanted chimney pieces. Press side pieces of chimney into frosting to form box. Hold a few minutes until set; let dry. Pipe frosting on bottom edges of chimney; place on roof.

PIPE any remaining frosting along roof lines, around base of chimney and around front corners of house and doors with writing tip #10 to create snowdrifts. Let set about 30 minutes.

GINGERBREAD CAKE COTTAGE

CUTTING AND ASSEMBLING GINGERBREAD CAKE COTTAGE

Cut cake into 3 pieces

Place piece 1 on tray; frost top. Frost top of piece 2; top with piece 3. Stand pieces 2 and 3 upright on piece 1 to form cottage.

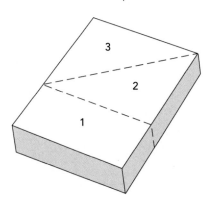

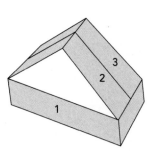

1 roll strawberry chewy fruit snack

1 roll grape chewy fruit snack

Cherry-Nut Cake (page 149)

Creamy Vanilla Frosting (page 151)

Assorted sugar sequins

Assorted colored sugars

Yellow food color

6 Party Blowers (page 61)

TIME-SAVER TIP: Substitute 1 package (1 lb 2.25 oz) white cake mix with pudding for the Cherry-Nut Cake. Prepare and bake as directed on package. Substitute 1¹/₂ tubs (1 lb each) vanilla ready-to-spread frosting for the Creamy Vanilla Frosting.

UNROLL and cut 12-inch piece from each fruit snack roll. Cut each piece lengthwise into 4 strips with a knife and a straightedge. Roll each strip in a spiral around handle of a wooden spoon. Store at room temperature at least 8 hours to set curl to make streamers.

BAKE Cherry-Nut Cake as directed for 2 rounds. Prepare Creamy Vanilla Frosting; reserve ¹/₄ cup for Party Blowers. Fill layers and frost cake. Press colored sugar sequins and sugars into frosting on side and along outer edge of top of cake.

TINT reserved frosting with 3 drops food coloring. Make party blowers. Place Party Blowers on top of cake with candy sticks toward center of cake. Unwrap streamers from spoon handles. Reshape into desired curl and place between Party Blowers and around base of cake.

Dark Cocoa Cake (page 147)
Fluffy Cocoa Frosting (page 152)
Tray or cardboard, 18 × 15 inches,
  covered

1 fresh rose or Gumdrop Rose
  (page 88)
Powdered Sugar
Chocolate Leaves (page 78)

TIME-SAVER TIP: Substitute 1 package (1 lb 2.25 oz) devil's food cake mix with pudding for the Dark Cocoa Cake. Prepare as directed on package and bake as directed in Dark Cocoa Cake.

BAKE Dark Cocoa Cake as directed for one 8-inch round and one 8-inch square. Prepare Fluffy Cocoa Frosting. Cut round layer in half. Arrange pieces on tray to form heart as shown in diagram. Frost cake, attaching pieces with small amount of frosting. Place fresh rose on frosting; sprinkled with powdered sugar. Arrange Chocolate Leaves next to stem.

CUTTING AND ASSEMBLING CHOCOLATE HEART CAKE

Cut round layer in half.

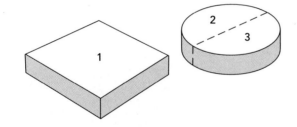

Place pieces, cut edges against sides of square layer, to form heart.

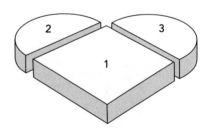

PARTY BLOWERS

For each blower, break a 5-inch candy stick in half. Cut a 4-inch piece from a roll of chewy fruit snack. Place a small amount of frosting $1/4$ inch from broken end of 1 candy stick half. Wrap narrow end of piece of fruit roll over frosting. Pipe 2 rows of frosting stars over seam with star tip #30. Curl the end of the fruit roll to about $1^1/2$ inches from star rows and secure with small amount of frosting if needed.

Cherry-Nut Cake (page 149)
Creamy Vanilla Frosting (page 151)
Red food color
Tray or cardboard, 16 × 12 inches, covered

Heart-shaped cookie cutters
Assorted nonpareils, colored sugars and sprinkles
3 ounces red cinnamon candies
Heart-shaped candies

HOW ABOUT a cake full of pumpkins, dinosaurs, bells, angels or stars? Use any shape cookie cutters and any color candy sprinkles for birthdays, hobbies, showers or holidays.

BAKE Cherry-Nut Cake as directed for 13 × 9-inch rectangle. Prepare Creamy Vanilla Frosting; reserve $^1/_2$ cup. Tint remaining frosting with 3 drops food color; reserve $^1/_2$ cup. Place cake on tray. Frost top and sides of cake.

PLACE various sizes of heart-shaped cookie cutters on cake. Sprinkle nonpareils, colored sugars and sprinkles inside cutters, pressing gently onto frosting. Carefully remove cookie cutters. Outline largest hearts with cinnamon candies. Place cinnamon candies along base of cake.

TINT reserved pink frosting with 3 additional drops food color. Place frosting in decorating bag with writing tip #4. Pipe beaded border around smaller hearts. Pipe beaded border along outside edge of cake with reserved white frosting. Add a few cinnamon candies or heart-shaped candies between hearts.

TIME-SAVER TIP: Substitute 1 package (1 lb 2.25 oz) white cake mix with pudding for the Cherry-Nut Cake. Prepare and bake as directed on package. Substitute 1$^1/_2$ tubs (1 lb each) vanilla ready-to-spread frosting for the Creamy Vanilla Frosting.

COOKIE CUTTER DESIGNS

Outlined Designs   **Press cookie cutters into frosted cake; outline markings with small candies. Or, dip cookie cutters in liquid food color; lightly press cutters into frosted cake.**

Filled-in Designs   **Place cookie cutters on frosted cake, sprinkle inside cutter with colored sugar, small candy sprinkles or small candies. Gently press into frosting; remove cookie cutters.**

CAKE FULL OF HEARTS AND CHOCOLATE HEART CAKE (PAGE 61)

Carrot Cake (page 146)

White Mountain Frosting (page 152)

Tray or cardboard, 12 × 8 inches, covered

1 cup flaked or shredded coconut

Jelly beans or small gumdrops

1 cup flaked or shredded coconut

Green food color

Pink construction paper

TIME-SAVER TIP: Substitute any 8- or 9-inch cake layer for the Carrot Cake. Substitute 1 package (7.2 ounces) fluffy white frosting mix for the White Mountain Frosting. Prepare as directed on package.

BAKE Carrot Cake as directed for 8- or 9-inch rounds. Reserve 1 layer for another use. Prepare White Mountain Frosting. Cut 1 layer in half as shown in diagram. Put halves together with frosting to form body. Place cake upright on cut edge on tray.

CUT a notch about one-third of the way up one edge of body to form head as shown in diagram. Attach cut-out piece for tail with toothpicks. Frost with remaining frosting, rounding body on sides. Sprinkle with 1 cup coconut. Cut ears from construction paper; press into top. Use jelly beans for eyes and nose.

SHAKE 1 cup shredded coconut and 3 drops food color in tightly covered jar until evenly tinted. Surround bunny with tinted coconut. Add additional jelly beans if desired.

CUTTING AND ASSEMBLING EASTER BUNNY CAKE

Cut layer in half. Put halves together to form body.

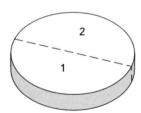

Cut notch about one-third of the way up one edge of body to form head.

Attach cut out piece for tail with toothpick.

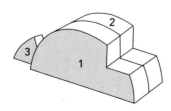

Cut 4 × 1³/₄-inch ears from pink construction paper. Fold as shown.

5 ounces almond paste

Red, green and yellow food colors

Purple paste food color

2 cups powdered sugar

2 tablespoons meringue powder

$^1/_4$ cup water

Almond Cake (page 149)

Creamy White Frosting (page 151)

TIME-SAVER TIP: Substitute 1 package (1 lb 2.25 oz) white cake mix with pudding for the Almond Cake. Prepare and bake as directed on package.

TO make lilies, knead and roll out half of the almond paste $^1/_8$ inch thick. Trace lily pattern (see bottom right, page 67); cut out 3 lilies. Holding lily in palm, gently roll into a cone shape, overlapping seam. Curl petals out and down. Dilute a few drops red food color with water. Brush red strips from the base up the center of each lily petal with a small brush. Roll a 1-inch ball of paste into a $2^1/_2$-inch bud. Knead 2 drops green food color into remaining almond paste. Roll out to $^1/_8$ inch thickness. Cut out 5 leaves about 3 inches long. Place on sheet of waxed paper, shaping to curl slightly. Allow lilies and leaves to dry at least 8 hours.

BEAT powdered sugar, meringue powder and water with standard mixer on medium speed or with hand mixer on high speed about 7 minutes or until stiff peaks form. Tint $^1/_2$ cup meringue icing with 3 drops yellow food color; reserve. Tint remaining icing with paste food color. Place purple icing in decorating bag with petal tip #190. Pipe 15 purple flowers onto waxed paper. Pipe 9 small purple flowers with petal tip #223. Pipe 18 stamens, about $1^3/_4$ inches long, with yellow icing and writing tip #4. Allow flowers and stamens to dry at least 8 hours. Store the decorating bag and tip with the yellow icing in an airtight container for cake assembly the next day.

BAKE Almond Cake as directed for 13 × 9-inch rectangle. Cut cake as shown. Freeze cut pieces uncovered about 1 hour for easier frosting if desired. Prepare Creamy White frosting. Tint $^1/_2$ cup frosting with 2 drops red food color. Tint $^1/_2$ cup frosting with 2 drops green food color.

ARRANGE cake pieces on tray to form cross as shown in diagram. Reserve $^1/_2$ cup of the white frosting. Frost top and sides with remaining white frosting. Spread a 1-inch-wide strip of pink frosting, $^1/_4$ inch thick, up the inside of decorating bag. Fill bag with reserved white frosting. Pipe shell border with star tip #32 along top edge and base of bake, holding bag so pink strip is toward the outside.

PIPE a small amount of yellow meringue icing inside each lily at the base; insert 5 stamens in icing in each lily. Place lilies and bud on cake. Place green frosting in decorating bag with writing tip #5. Pipe stems to each lily; pipe long stem along left side of cake. Arrange leaves along stem.

ARRANGE large and small purple flowers on top of cake. Pipe small flowers to fill in with remaining pink frosting and star tip #18. Pipe leaves around some of the flowers with green frosting and leaf tip #67. Pipe a small dot of yellow icing in center of each flower.

EASTER CROSS CAKE

CUTTING AND ASSEMBLING EASTER CROSS CAKE

Cut cake lengthwise into 2 strips. Cut a 4-inch-long piece from wider strip.

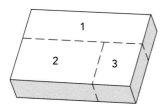

Arrange pieces to form cross.

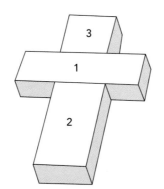

Trace lily pattern. Enlarge if desired.

POT-O'-GOLD CAKE

PASTE FOOD color gives the bright, sharp colors needed for the rainbow. Liquid food color will have a softer look.

Applesauce Cake (page 145)
Creamy White Frosting (page 151)
Red, yellow, blue and green paste food colors
2 tablespoons cocoa
Tray or cardboard, 18 × 14 inches, covered

1/3 cup shredded coconut
Green liquid food color
8 butterscotch hard candies, crushed
60 small round green candies

TIME-SAVER TIP: Substitute 1 package (1 lb 2.25 oz) yellow cake mix with pudding for the Applesauce Cake. Prepare and bake as directed on package. Substitute 2 tubs (1 lb each) vanilla ready-to-spread frosting for the Creamy White Frosting.

BAKE Applesauce Cake as directed for 13 × 9-inch rectangle. Cut cake as shown in diagram. Freeze cut pieces uncovered about 1 hour for easier frosting if desired. Prepare Creamy White Frosting. Tint 2 cups frosting red with paste color and 1 cup frosting each yellow, blue and green with paste colors. Mix cocoa and remaining 1 cup frosting.

ARRANGE cake pieces on tray to form rainbow, pot and grass as shown in diagram. Frost top edge and side of the rainbow with red frosting. Frost the center with yellow frosting. Frost bottom edge and side with blue frosting. Frost top of the pot yellow. Draw a fork through frosting, following curve of rainbow.

RESERVE 1/4 cup cocoa frosting; frost pot with remaining frosting. Pipe a band of frosting to make the pot edge with reserved cocoa frosting and petal tip #104. Repeat 2 more times over the bands to form a ridge.

SHAKE coconut and 2 drops green liquid food color in tightly covered jar until evenly tinted. Reserve 1/4 cup green frosting; frost the grass piece with remaining frosting. Sprinkle with tinted coconut. Stack the butterscotch pieces above the pot. Pipe shamrock stems at random on cake top with reserved green frosting and writing tip #4. Pipe four dots of frosting at one end of each stem. Place the green candies on the frosting dots to form shamrocks.

POT-O'-GOLD CAKE

CUTTING AND ASSEMBLING POT-O'-GOLD CAKE

Cut cake to form rainbow, pot and grass.

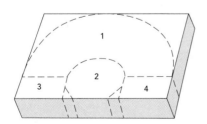

Arrange pieces to form pot at end of the rainbow.

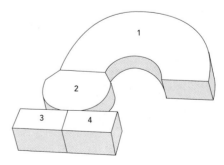

FIRECRACKER CAKES

TIME-SAVER TIP: Substitute
1 package (1 lb 2.25 oz) devil's
food cake mix with pudding for the
Chocolate-Cherry Cake. Prepare
and bake as directed on package.
Substitute 1½ tubs (1 lb each)
vanilla ready-to-spread frosting for
the Creamy Vanilla Frosting.

Chocolate-Cherry Cake (page 147)
Creamy Vanilla Frosting
  (page 151)

Red food color
About 12 blue birthday candles

BAKE Chocolate-Cherry Cake as directed for cupcakes. Prepare
Creamy Vanilla Frosting. Tint 2 cups frosting with 6 drops food
color. Put 2 cupcakes together end-to-end with small amount red
frosting. Frost sides of firecrackers with red frosting. Frost ends
with white frosting. Insert a birthday candle in one end of each firecracker to resemble wick.

PRESIDENT'S DAY DESIGN

Gumdrop Hatchets **For each hatchet, roll 1 large red gumdrop on heavily sugared surface into oval
¹/₈ inch thick (left). Cut hatchet as shown (right). Prepare Mini Bûche de Noël Cakes (page 55). Substitute
Gumdrop Hatchets for Gumdrop Holly.**

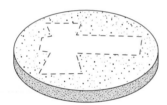
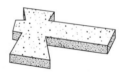

JACK-O'-LANTERN CAKE

Pumpkin-Gingerbread Cake (page 148)
Creamy White Frosting (page 151)
Red and yellow food colors
Tray or cardboard, 10 inches round, covered
1 green flat-bottom ice-cream cone

1 teaspoon sugar
10 large black gumdrops or 1 milk chocolate candy bar (1.55 ounces)
1 tube (.68 ounce) green decorating gel, if desired
Spearmint leaves, if desired

MAKE A face on the other side of the jack-o'-lantern with candy corn and shoe-string licorice, or pipe on chocolate or black frosting.

BAKE Pumpkin-Gingerbread Cake as directed for two 1 1/2-quart casseroles. Prepare Creamy White Frosting. Tint with 6 drops each red and yellow food colors.

TRIM tops of layers to make flat if necessary. Place 1 layer, rounded side down, on tray. Spread with 1/3 cup frosting. Place remaining layer, rounded side up, on top to make pumpkin. Frost with orange frosting. Make vertical lines over cake with knife to shape pumpkin. Trim cone to desired height for stem; place upside down on cake.

SPRINKLE 1 teaspoon sugar on piece of waxed paper. Place gumdrops about 1/4 inch apart on sugar. Top with another piece of waxed paper. Roll gumdrops between waxed paper to 1/4-inch thickness. Cut eyes, nose and mouth. Arrange on pumpkin for face. Or cut candy bar into two large triangles for eyes and 7 small triangles for nose and mouth. Arrange on pumpkin for face. Decorate as desired with vines and leaves.

TIME-SAVER TIP: Substitute 2 tubs (1 lb each) vanilla ready-to-spread frosting for the Creamy White Frosting.

BLACK CAT CAKE

Dark Cocoa Cake (page 147)
Creamy Cocoa Frosting (page 151)
Tray or cardboard, 18 × 12 inches,
    covered

2 large yellow gumdrops
1 small black gumdrop
Black shoestring licorice

TIME-SAVER TIP: Substitute
1 package (1 lb 2.25 oz) devil's
food cake mix with pudding for the
Dark Cocoa Cake. Prepare and
bake as directed on package.
Substitute $1\frac{1}{2}$ tubs (1 lb each)
chocolate ready-to-spread frosting
for the Creamy Cocoa Frosting.

BAKE Dark Cocoa Cake as directed for 8- to 9-inch rounds. Cut 1
layer as shown in diagram. Freeze cut pieces uncovered about 1
hour for easier frosting if desired. Prepare Creamy Cocoa Frosting.
Arrange uncut layer and the pieces on tray to form cat as shown in
diagram.

FROST cake, attaching pieces with small amount of frosting. Cut
slice off bottom of each yellow gumdrop; use slices for eyes. Use
black gumdrop for nose and shoestring licorice for whiskers and
lines on eyes and front paws.

CUTTING AND ASSEMBLING BLACK CAT CAKE

Cut one layer to form head, ears and tail of cat.

Arrange pieces around uncut layer to form cat.

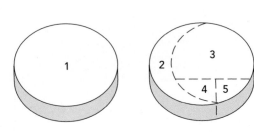

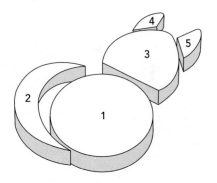

FOR A Christmas cake, substitute red- or green-tinted White Chocolate Glaze (page 153) for the Chocolate Glaze and decorate with Gumdrop Holly (page 55).

Chocolate Angel Food Cake
   (page 145)
Chocolate Glaze (page 153)

¹/4 cup powdered sugar
1 to 2 teaspoons hot water
Gumdrop Spider (page 75)

BAKE Chocolate Angel Food Cake as directed. Spread with Chocolate Glaze, letting glaze run down side unevenly. Mix powdered sugar and water until smooth and of drizzling consistency. Using a teaspoon and turning the plate as you work, drizzle white glaze in circles, beginning with small circle in center and encircling with larger rings ¹/2 inch apart. Immediately draw a knife from the center outward 8 times, equally spaced to make web (see page 75). Attach Gumdrop Spider to cake with toothpick.

TIME-SAVER TIP: Substitute 1 package (1 lb) white angel food cake mix for the Chocolate Angel Food Cake. Prepare and bake as directed on package, except add 2 tablespoons cocoa to dry mix.

SPIDERWEB CAKE

HALLOWEEN HAUNTERS

These Halloween "tricks" make cakes and cupcakes irresistible!

Gumdrop Spider   For each spider, roll 1 large black gumdrop on heavily sugared surface into oval $1/8$ inch thick. Cut into desired spider shape. Place on cake or cupcakes with Web design.

Marshmallow Ghosts   For each ghost, cut 1 large marshmallow in half, crosswise. Attach 1 marshmallow half cut side down to top of whole marshmallow with a small amount of White Mountain Frosting (page 152) to form head. (Use other half of marshmallow for another ghost.) Press 2 chocolate chips into head for eyes. Make 4 small cuts in each of 2 miniature marshmallows to form fingers; flatten slightly. Attach hands to ghost with frosting. Arrange ghosts on top of cake frosted with White Mountain Frosting, bringing frosting up around bottoms so ghosts appear to be coming from frosting. Dab a small amount of frosting on top of ghosts.

Gumdrop Cat   For each cat, cut a large black gumdrop into 3 pieces as shown. Use small rounded top piece for head and largest bottom piece for body. Cut tail and ears from middle piece. Arrange to form cat.

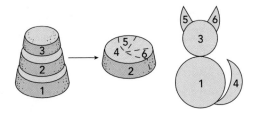

CHOCOLATE WEB DESIGN

Drizzle round frosted or glazed cake with melted chocolate, beginning with small circle in center and encircling with larger circle, $1/2$ inch outside the other. Immediately draw a knife from center outward 8 times, equally spaced.

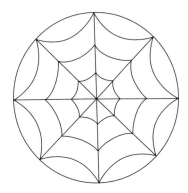

TIME-SAVER TIP: Substitute 1 package (1 lb 2.25 oz) yellow cake mix with pudding for the Yellow Cake. Prepare and bake as directed on package. Substitute 1½ tubs (1 lb each) vanilla ready-to-spread frosting for the Creamy Vanilla Frosting and ½ tub (1-lb size) chocolate ready-to-spread frosting for the Chocolate Decorator Frosting.

Yellow Cake (page 150)
Creamy Vanilla Frosting (page 151)
Chocolate Decorator Frosting (page 150)

Blue, yellow and orange sugars
1 gummy worm candy
Candy corn
1 chocolate chip

BAKE Yellow Cake as directed for two 9-inch rounds. Cut 1 layer as shown in diagram. Freeze cut pieces uncovered about 1 hour for easier frosting. Prepare Creamy Vanilla Frosting.

PLACE uncut layer on cake plate; frost top and side. Place circle on larger layer, ½ inch from bottom edge; frost. Arrange head and shoulders on circle; frost. Prepare Chocolate Decorator Frosting. Dip fork into chocolate frosting and lightly drag through Creamy Vanilla Frosting to form feathers around both layers and on shoulders.

SPRINKLE blue sugar on head, yellow sugar on edge of small layer and orange sugar on edge of larger layer. Cut gummy worm in half. Place 1 candy corn on head for beak. Use gummy worm for turkey's wattle. Use chocolate chip for eye. Use candy corn for claws and feathers.

CUTTING AND ASSEMBLING TURKEY GOBBLER CAKE

Cut one layer to form body, head and shoulders.

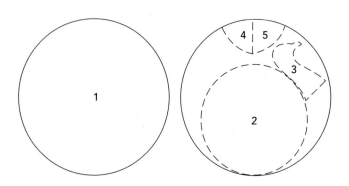

Place uncut layer on plate; frost. Place piece 2 on top about 1/2-inch from bottom edge; frost. Arrange pieces 3, 4 and 5 on body.

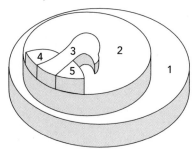

TURKEY GOBBLER CAKE AND THANKSGIVING CAKE (PAGE 78)

THANKSGIVING CAKE

When buying the fruit-shaped candies for the Cornucopia Garnishes, pick up an ounce or two more to sprinkle around the base of the cake.

TIME-SAVER TIP: Substitute 1 package (1 lb 2.25 oz) spice cake mix with pudding for the Apple Cake. Prepare and bake as directed on package. Substitute 1 1/2 tubs (1 lb each) cream cheese ready-to-spread frosting for the Cream Cheese Frosting.

Apple Cake (page 146)
Cream Cheese Frosting (page 151)
1 tablespoon cocoa

Tray or cardboard, 16 × 12 inches, covered
Cornucopia Garnishes (below)

BAKE Apple Cake as directed for 13 × 9-inch rectangle. Prepare Cream Cheese Frosting. Mix 1/4 cup frosting and the cocoa. Spread a 1-inch-wide stripe of cocoa frosting, 1/4 inch thick, up the inside of decorating bag with star tip #30. Place 1 cup cream cheese frosting in bag. Place cake on tray. Frost cake with remaining frosting. Pipe shell border around top and base of cake, holding bag so chocolate stripe is toward the outside.

ARRANGE Cornucopia Garnishes in 3 rows on top of cake, pointing tips in opposite directions every other row. Sprinkle cake lightly with remaining sugar mixture from Cornucopia Garnishes if desired. Arrange additional fruit candies around bottom border if desired.

CORNUCOPIA GARNISHES

Mix 2 tablespoons sugar and 1/4 teaspoon ground cinnamon in plastic bag; reserve. Drizzle 1 teaspoon melted margarine over 12 horn-shaped corn snacks, stirring until well coated. Toss corn snacks in sugar mixture. Just before serving, place cornucopias on cake. Arrange about 5 ounces small fruit-shaped candies at openings of cornucopias for fruit spilling out. (See photo of Thanksgiving Cake on page 77.)

CHOCOLATE LEAVES

Wash and dry 12 to 18 fresh nonpoisonous (unsprayed) leaves (such as lemon, grape or rose leaves) or pliable plastic leaves. Melt 2 ounces white chocolate (white baking bar), 1/2 cup (3 ounces) semisweet chocolate chips or 2 squares (1 ounce each) semisweet chocolate and 1 teaspoon shortening. (See page 143 for Chocolate Tips.) Brush chocolate about 1/8 inch thick over backs of leaves using small brush. Refrigerate until firm, at least 1 hour. Peel off leaves, handling as little as possible. Refrigerate chocolate leaves until ready to use. (See photo of Chocolate Heart Cake on page 62.)

Two-tone Chocolate Leaves Melt 1/2 cup butterscotch-flavored chips and 1 teaspoon shortening. Drizzle on the backs of leaves with a spoon; let dry. Brush melted chocolate as directed above evenly over butterscotch, completely covering backs of leaves. (See photo of Fall Angel Food Cake on page 79.)

Spicy Angel Food Cake (page 145)
1 1/2 cups whipping (heavy) cream
1/3 cup packed brown sugar
1 teaspoon vanilla

1/2 teaspoon pumpkin pie spice
Two-tone Chocolate Leaves (page 78)
Orange peel

TIME-SAVER TIP: Substitute 1 package (1 lb) white angel food cake mix for the Spicy Angel Food Cake. Prepare and bake as directed on package—except add 1 teaspoon pumpkin pie spice during last 30 seconds of beating.

BAKE Spicy Angel Food Cake as directed. Beat whipping cream, brown sugar, vanilla and pumpkin pie spice in chilled bowl until stiff. Frost side and top of cake. Refrigerate until serving time.

GARNISH with Two-tone Chocolate Leaves and orange peel just before serving. Refrigerate any remaining cake.

FALL ANGEL FOOD CAKE

SPINNING THE dreidel is a traditional Hanukkah game. This fun cake, made in the shape of a dreidel, will be a delightful addition to your celebration of the Jewish Festival of Lights.

TIME-SAVER TIP: Substitute 1 package (1 lb 2.25 oz) white cake mix with pudding for the Hazelnut Cake. Prepare and bake as directed on package. Substitute 2 tubs (1 lb each) vanilla ready-to-spread frosting for the Creamy White Frosting.

Hazelnut Cake (page 149)
Creamy White Frosting (page 151)
Blue food color
1 teaspoon cocoa

Tray or cardboard, 20 × 12 inches, covered
About 1/2 cup miniature chocolate chips

BAKE Hazelnut Cake as directed for 13 × 9-inch rectangle. Cut cake as shown in diagram. Freeze cut pieces uncovered about 1 hour for easier frosting if desired. Prepare Creamy White Frosting. Tint one-half of the frosting with 8 drops food color. Mix cocoa and 1/4 cup of the white frosting.

ARRANGE pieces on tray to form dreidel as shown in diagram. Reserve 2/3 cup white frosting; frost the center and sides of the dreidel with remaining frosting. Reserve 2/3 cup blue frosting; frost the dreidel point, handle top and sides with the remaining frosting, attaching pieces with small amount of frosting. Outline the Hebrew letter of your choice with a toothpick. Fill in with cocoa frosting; outline with chocolate chips.

PLACE reserved white frosting in decorating bag with star tip #32. Pipe a shell border along base and top edge of white-frosted cake. Pipe a shell border along base and top edge of blue frosted cake with blue frosting and shell tip. Outline top borders with chocolate chips if desired.

HANUKKAH DREIDEL CAKE

CUTTING AND ASSEMBLING HANUKKAH DREIDEL CAKE

Cut cake to form body and handle of dreidel.

Arrange pieces to form dreidel.

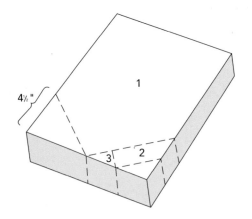

4½"

1

3   2

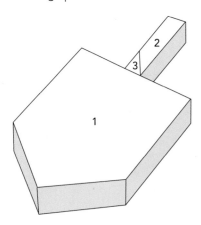

2

3

1

THREE

Celebration Cakes

Classic White Wedding Cake *84*

Apricot-Almond Wedding Cake *86*

Petits Fours *89*

Anniversary Cake *90*

Double-Ring Shower Cake *90*

Umbrella Cake *92*

Baby Bib Shower Cake *94*

Bootie Shower Cakes *95*

"Birthday-saurus" Bash Cake *96*

Flower Silhouette Birthday Cake *98*

Happy Birthday Cake *98*

Mother's Day Straw Hat Cake *100*

Father's Day T-Shirt Cake *102*

Computer Cake *105*

Gone Fishin' Cake *106*

Housewarming Cake *106*

Star of David Cake *108*

Classic White Wedding Cake (page 84)

PREPARE CREAMY White Frosting and White Decorator Frosting using clear vanilla to keep the frosting white. Prepare as many recipes of the decorating frosting as nessesary. Prepare batter just before baking; measure ingredients ahead if desired. Bake cake layers the day before they are to be assembled, or bake them earlier and freeze.

6 recipes White Cake (page 149)
2 recipes Creamy White Frosting (page 151)
Large tray, mirror or aluminum-foil covered cardboard, 16 inches round
Aluminum foil-covered cardboard, 10 inches round
Aluminum foil-covered cardboard, 6 inches round
White Decorator Frosting (page 152)

GREASE and flour 1 round pan, 10 × 2 inches. Prepare 1 recipe White Cake. Pour $4^1/2$ cups batter into pan. Bake 45 to 50 minutes or until top springs back when touched lightly in center. Cool 15 minutes; remove from pan. Cool completely.

GREASE and flour 1 round pan, 14 × 2 inches, and 1 round pan, 6 × 2 inches. Prepare 2 recipes White Cake, 1 recipe at a time. Pour $1^1/2$ cups batter into 6-inch pan and $7^3/4$ cups batter into 14-inch pan. Bake 6-inch layer 35 to 40 minutes, 14-inch layer 50 to 55 minutes or until top springs back when touched lightly in center. Cool 15 minutes; remove from pans. Cool completely.

REPEAT above process, making a total of 6 layers. Each tier of wedding cake will consist of 2 layers. (Height must measure 3 inches total or $1^1/2$ inches per layer.) Tops of layers should be flat for ease in stacking. Slice off rounded tops if necessary.

PREPARE 1 recipe Creamy White Frosting. Place one 14-inch layer on tray. Frost top using 1 cup frosting; top with remaining 14-inch layer. Frost side and top with remaining frosting. Place covered 10-inch cardboard circle on first tier; place 10-inch layer on cardboard.

PREPARE 1 recipe Creamy White Frosting. Frost top using $3/4$ cup frosting; top with remaining 10-inch layer. Frost side and top using 2 cups frosting. Place covered 6-inch cardboard circle on second tier; place 6-inch layer on cardboard. Frost top using $1/3$ cup frosting; top with remaining 6-inch layer. Frost side and top with remaining frosting.

PREPARE White Decorator Frosting, 1 recipe at a time. Place in decorating bag with petal tip #103. Make desired number of roses (see How To Make Roses on page 142); refrigerate until ready to use. Pipe shell border around top edge and base of each tier with open star tip #18. Arrange roses on cake as desired. Pipe vines with writing tip #4 and leaves with leaf tip #352 onto roses. Top with fresh flowers if desired (see Fresh Flower Decorations on page 88).

How to Cut a Round Tiered Wedding Cake

Use a thin, sharp or serrated knife. Insert knife into cake, keeping point down and handle up. Slice, pulling knife toward you. If frosting sticks, dip knife in hot water or wipe with damp paper towel after cutting each slice.

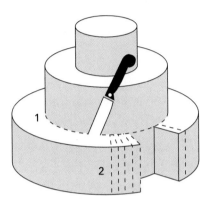

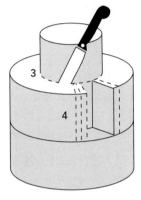

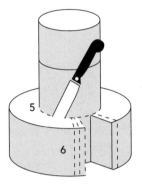

Cut vertically through bottom layer at edge of second layer as indicated by dotted line 1; then cut into wedges as indicated by dotted line 2.

Follow same procedure with middle layer by cutting vertically through second layer at edge of top layer as indicated by dotted line 3; then cut into wedges as indicated by dotted line 4.

Return to bottom layer and cut along dotted line 5; cut into wedges as indicated by dotted line 6. Separate remaining layers (traditionally the top layer is frozen for the couple's first anniversary); cut as desired.

Wedding Cake Yields — Servings per 2-Layer Tier

Each serving measures 2 × 1 inch from a tier 3 inches high.

Layer	Round	Square
6 inches	10	18
7 inches	15	—
8 inches	22	32
9 inches	28	40
10 inches	35	50
12 inches	50	72
14 inches	70	98
16 inches	100	128
18 x 12-inch rectangle		108

Baking Different Sizes

Layers other than sizes baked for Classic White Wedding Cake (page 84) can be made. One recipe White Cake yields about 5 cups batter.

Pan Size	Amount of Batter	Baking Time
7 x 2-inch round	2 cups	40 to 45 minutes
8 x 2-inch round	2½ cups	40 to 45 minutes
9 x 2-inch round	3 cups	45 to 50 minutes
12 x 2-inch round	5 cups	45 to 50 minutes

FOR THE entire wedding cake, prepare 3 recipes Almond Cake and 2 recipes Creamy White Frosting, using almond extract. Edible glitter is available at specialty cake decorating stores. Prepare batter just before baking; measure ingredients ahead if desired. Bake cake layers the day before they are to be assembled, or bake them earlier and freeze.

3 recipes Almond Cake (page 149)
2 packages (6 ounces each) premier white baking bars
2 recipes Creamy White Frosting (page 151)
Red and yellow food colors
Large tray, mirror or aluminum foil-covered cardboard, 14 inches round

1¹/₄ cups apricot fruit spread
Aluminum foil-covered cardboard, 9 inches round
White edible glitter, if desired
Chocolate Leaves (page 78)
Chocolate Twigs (page 144)
Apricot Rose (page 88)

GREASE and flour 2 round pans, 9 × 1¹/₂ inches. Prepare 1 recipe Almond Cake. Pour into pans. Bake 30 to 35 minutes or until top springs back when touched lightly in center. Cool 15 minutes; remove from pan. Cool completely.

GREASE and flour 1 round pan, 12 × 2 inches. Prepare 1 recipe Almond Cake. Pour into pan. Bake 45 to 50 minutes or until top springs back when touched lightly in center. Cool 15 minutes; remove from pan. Cool completely. Repeat.

EACH tier of wedding cake will consist of 2 layers. Tops of layers should be flat for ease in stacking. Slice off rounded tops if necessary.

PREPARE white chocolate ribbons, using white baking bars, as directed for Chocolate Ribbons (page 144). Place ribbons on cookie sheet; set aside. (It is important that these be prepared before frosting the cake because they will not adhere to frosting once it is set.)

PREPARE 1 recipe Creamy White Frosting. Tint with 2 drops red and 6 drops yellow food color. Place one 12-inch layer on tray. Spread ³/₄ cup fruit spread evenly over layer. Top with remaining 12-inch layer. Frost side and top. Place 9-inch cardboard circle on first tier.

PREPARE 1 recipe Creamy White Frosting. Tint with 2 drops red and 6 drops yellow food color. Place one 9-inch layer on cardboard. Spread ¹/₂ cup fruit spread evenly over layer. Top with remaining layer. Frost side and top. Gently press ribbons into side and top of tier. Sprinkle with white edible glitter. Decorate with Chocolate Leaves and Chocolate Twigs made from white chocolate and Apricot Rose.

APRICOT-ALMOND WEDDING CAKE

CAKES IN BLOOM

Springtime, or any time, add the elegance and simplicity of flowers to your cakes with these fresh flower ideas and beautifully crafted look-alikes.

Gumdrop Rose   Roll 4 large red gumdrops on well-sugared surface into ovals $1/8$ inch thick as shown. Sprinkle with sugar. Cut ovals into halves. Roll 1 half-oval tightly to form center of rose. Place more half-ovals around center, overlapping slightly. Press together at base; trim base. Roll out green gumdrops to cut leaves if desired.

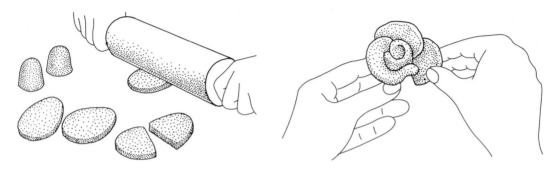

Apricot Rose   Follow directions above for Gumdrop Rose, except use dried apricot halves.

Fresh Flower Decorations   Fresh edible flowers can enhance the attractiveness of a cake. Select fresh flowers that can last out of water for several hours without wilting. Or, insert ends of flowers in watering tubes. Buttercups, carnations, chrysanthemums, daisies, pansies, roses and violets are all good choices. Request unsprayed flowers when ordering. If you think flowers may have been sprayed with a pesticide, dip them in soapy water, rinse and dry before placing on cake. A small piece of plastic wrap also can be placed beneath the flowers that will touch the cake. Accent with baby's breath or greenery such as ferns. (See photo of Classic White Wedding Cake on page 82.)

Sugared Roses   Dip small fresh roses in water, rinse and pat dry. Trim stems to about 2 inches. Mix 2 tablespoons light corn syrup and 1 teaspoon water. Brush mixture on rose petals with small, soft brush, separating petals as you coat them. Sift or sprinkle superfine or granulated sugar lightly on roses, shaking gently to remove excess sugar. Other flowers that can be sugared are bachelor buttons, carnations, chrysanthemums, small orchids, sweet peas and violets. Do not eat flowers. (See photo of Chocolate Heart Cake on page 62.)

Whipped Cream Rosettes   Whip 1 cup whipping cream and 2 tablespoons powdered sugar. Pipe rosettes (see How To Make Rosettes on page 138) onto wax paper-lined cookie sheet. Freeze until firm; carefully remove from waxed paper. Wrap and store in freezer. Use to decorate cakes that will be cut and served or place on individual serving as they are cut. (See photo of Walnut Torte on page 123.)

PETITS FOURS

White Cake (page 149)
Petits Fours Glaze (page 153)
2 cups powdered sugar
2 to 3 tablespoons water

BAKE White Cake as directed for jellyroll pan. Cut cake into 1^1/$_2$-inch squares, rounds, diamonds or hearts.

PLACE cakes, one at a time, on wire rack over large bowl. Pour enough Petits Fours Glaze over top to cover top and sides. (Glaze can be reheated and used again.)

MIX powdered sugar and just enough water to make a frosting that holds its shape. Place frosting in decorating bag with writing tip #3. Decorate as desired. *About 54 pieces.*

TIME-SAVER TIP: Substitute 1 package (1 lb 2.25 oz) white cake mix with pudding. Prepare as directed on package except bake as directed in White Cake recipe for jellyroll pan.

ANNIVERSARY CAKE

THIS PRETTY and unusual cake will also be perfect for showers, birthdays and as a small wedding cake.

Pastel Marble Cake (page 149)
Buttercream Frosting (page 150)

BAKE Pastel Marble Cake as directed for 13 × 9-inch rectangle. Prepare Buttercream Frosting; reserve $3^1/2$ cups. Frost cake with remaining frosting. Mark a 2-inch border around top edge of cake. Place $^2/3$ cup at a time of the reserved frosting in decorating bag with star tip #18. Pipe diagonal lines inside border; repeat at opposite diagonal. Pipe shell borders around top and bottom edges of cake and inside border.

PIPE message in center of cake. Decorate with Fresh Flower Decorations (page 88) if desired.

TIME-SAVER TIP: Substitute 1 package (1 lb 2.25 oz) white cake mix with pudding for the Pastel Marble Cake. Prepare and bake as directed on package—except tint batter and spoon into pan as directed in recipe.

MARSHMALLOW FLOWERS

For every 3 flowers, snip 3 pink miniature marshmallows into thirds, make sure not to cut entirely through marshmallows. Fan marshmallow pieces out. Snip 1 green miniature marshmallow into 3 pieces. Attach 1 green piece to each pink flower by pressing gently in place. Press a silver nonpareil in center of each flower. (Spray hands and scissors with vegetable cooking spray to keep marshmallows from sticking.) Remove silver nonpareils before eating.

DOUBLE-RING SHOWER CAKE

THIS DOUBLE-ring cake does double (or even triple) duty! Use it for wedding showers, anniversaries or as a small wedding cake.

2 recipes Almond Cake (page 149)
32 Marshmallow Flowers (bottom left)
Creamy White Frosting (page 151)
Red food color
Tray or cardboard, 24 × 14 inches, covered

BAKE 1 recipe Almond Cake as directed for 12-cup ring mold; repeat. Prepare Marshmallow Flowers; set aside.

PREPARE Creamy White Frosting. Tint $^1/2$ cup with 2 drops food color; reserve. Cut cake as shown in diagram. Arrange pieces on tray to form double-ring as shown in diagram. Frost cake, attaching pieces with small amount of frosting.

PLACE reserved pink frosting in decorating bag with star tip #18. Pipe shell border around outside and inside base of rings. Mark half circles around upper outside edge of cake rings with 2-inch diameter glass (or with ruler and toothpick). Pipe swag border around cake, following scalloped markings with writing tip #4. Place Marshmallow Flower where swag border touches top edge of cake. Place flowers around inside edges of rings about every 2 inches.

TIME-SAVER TIP: Substitute 2 packaged (1 lb 2.25 oz each) white cake mix with pudding for the 2 recipes Almond Cake. Prepare and bake as directed for 12-cup ovenproof ring mold. Substitute 2 tubs (1 lb each) vanilla ready-to-spread frosting for the Creamy White Frosting.

ANNIVERSARY CAKE AND DOUBLE-RING SHOWER CAKE

CUTTING AND ASSEMBLING DOUBLE-RING SHOWER CAKE

Cut piece from side of one ring cake to fit arc of second ring cake.

Join rings together, fitting uncut ring cake into cut section of ring cake.

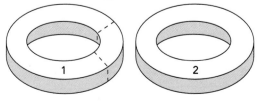

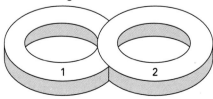

UMBRELLA CAKE

TIME-SAVER TIP: Substitute 1 package (1 lb 2.25 oz) lemon cake mix with pudding for the Lemon–Poppy Seed Cake. Prepare and bake as directed for 2 heart pans in Lemon–Poppy Seed recipe. Substitute 2 packages (7.2 ounce each) fluffy white frosting mix for the Fluffy Citrus Frosting. Prepare as directed on package. Tint with yellow food color.

Lemon–Poppy Seed Cake (page 150)
Fluffy Citrus Frosting (page 152)
Yellow food color
Tray or cardboard, 22 × 18 inches, covered

Pastel candy-coated chocolate candies
Ribbon, for bow

BAKE Lemon–Poppy Seed cake as directed for 2 heart pans. Cut cake as shown in diagram. Freeze uncovered about 1 hour for easier frosting if desired. Prepare Fluffy Citrus Frosting, using lemon peel; reserve $1^1/2$ cups. Tint remaining frosting with 8 drops food color.

ARRANGE cake pieces on tray to form umbrella as shown in diagram, trimming pieces 2 and 3 for handle. Frost top of umbrella with yellow frosting and handle with white frosting, attaching pieces with small amount of frosting. Decorate with candy-coated chocolate candies. Attach bow at handle.

CUTTING AND ASSEMBLING UMBRELLA CAKE

Cut one heart cake in half.

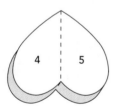

Cut a piece from each side of second heart cake, matching the length of cuts.

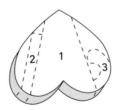

Trim pieces 2 and 3 for handle. Arrange pieces to form umbrella.

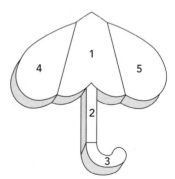

ALMOND FLOWERS

For each flower, place tips of 5 sliced almonds in frostings to form a flower using almonds as the petals. Pipe a drop of frosting in the center with a small star tip. Or, place small candy in center.

BABY BIB SHOWER CAKE

Hazelnut Cake (page 149)
Creamy Vanilla Frosting (page 151)

Red and blue food colors
Pastel candy mints

TIME-SAVER TIP: Substitute 1 package (1 lb 2.25 oz) white cake mix with pudding for the Hazelnut Cake. Prepare and bake as directed on package. Substitute 1 1/2 tubs (1 lb each) vanilla ready-to-spread frosting for the Creamy Vanilla Frosting.

BAKE Hazelnut Cake as directed for two 8- or 9-inch rounds. Prepare Creamy Vanilla Frosting; reserve 1 cup. Fill and frost cake with remaining frosting. Make vertical lines on side of cake with decorating comb or tines of fork if desired.

PLACE 1/2 cup reserved frosting in decorating bag with petal tip #124. Pipe ruffle around outer top edge of cake, leaving 3-inch opening at top.

TINT two-thirds of remaining frosting with 2 drops blue food color. Pipe outer border of bib with blue frosting and writing tip #5. Pipe inner opening of bib about 3 inches in diameter; join circles with tie at top. Make small bows on bib and write desired message in bib opening. Tint remaining frosting with 2 drops of red food color; pipe dots between bows. Arrange mints around base of cake.

BABY BIB SHOWER CAKE AND BOOTIE SHOWER CAKES

White Cake (page 149)
White Mountain Frosting
(page 152)

Food colors, if desired
Striped fruit-flavored chewing gum

TINT THE booties pastel yellow, blue or pink for a traditional look or bright colors for a fun, contemporary look.

BAKE White Cake as directed for cupcakes. Remove paper baking cups. Place 2 cupcakes upside down on separate plates. Cut small piece off side of a third cupcake to form flat surface. Cut third cupcake horizontally in half. Place one half with cut side against cupcake on plate to form bootie as shown in diagram. Place remaining half against second cupcake. Repeat with remaining cupcakes.

PREPARE White Mountain Frosting; reserve ²/₃ cup. Tint remaining frosting if desired. Frost booties, attaching pieces with small amount of frosting. Place reserved frosting in decorating bag with writing tip #4. Outline top and tongue of booties with frosting. Cut chewing gum into strips for accents and lace; place on booties.

TIME-SAVER TIP: Substitute 1 package (1 lb 2.25 oz) white cake mix with pudding for the White Cake. Prepare and bake as directed on package. Substitute 2 packages (7.2 ounces each) fluffy white frosting mix for the White Mountain Frosting. Prepare as directed on package.

CUTTING AND ASSEMBLING BOOTIE SHOWER CAKES

Cut piece off side of one cupcake.

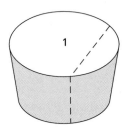

Cut cupcake horizontally in half.

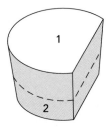

Place halves with cut sides against two other cupcakes.

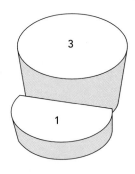

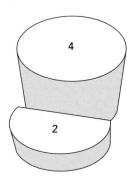

LOOK FOR cookies that have opposites in the package so you can get matching "pairs" to make the front and back of each dinosaur.

TIME-SAVER TIP: Substitute 1 package (1 lb 2.25 oz) yellow cake mix with pudding for the Apple Cake. Prepare and bake as directed on package. Substitute 2 tubs (1 lb each) vanilla ready-to-spread frosting for the Creamy White frosting.

16 spearmint leaves
Apple Cake (page 146)
Tray or cardboard, 16 × 2 inches, covered
Creamy White Frosting (page 151)

Red, yellow and green food colors
4 pretzel rods
6 dinosaur-shaped cookies (2 each of three different shapes)
Dinosaur-shaped candy sprinkles

ROLL spearmint leaves to $^1/8$-inch thickness. Trim, if necessary, to retain leaf shape. Snip edges to resemble palm leaves. Quickly dip in cool water. Allow to dry on wire rack at least 24 hours to stiffen.

BAKE Apple Cake as directed for 13 × 9-inch rectangle. Place cake on tray. Prepare Creamy White Frosting. Tint $^1/4$ cup frosting with 2 drops red food color and $^1/2$ cup frosting with 3 drops yellow food color. Tint remaining frosting with 8 drops green food color.

PLACE pink frosting in decorating bag with writing tip #4. Pipe detail lines on fronts of 1 set of dinosaur cookies. Pipe detail lines on fronts of the other 2 sets of cookies with yellow frosting and writing tip. Attach 4 leaves together with small amount of green frosting.

RESERVE $^3/4$ cup green frosting; frost cake with remaining frosting. Pipe shell border around top and base of cake with reserved green frosting and star tip #32; sprinkle with dinosaur-shaped candy sprinkles. Break off about 2 inches from each pretzel for tree trunks. Arrange on cake, pushing broken end of pretzel all the way through cake. Pipe stars around base of each trunk to anchor.

WRITE name on top of cake with yellow frosting and writing tip #4. Decorate with dinosaur-shaped candy sprinkles as desired. Attach cookie sets back to back with small amount of frosting. Slide 2 flat toothpicks between the cookies at the base about 1 inch apart to serve as standing supports. Place on cake. Attach leaves to trunks with small amount of green frosting. Decorate with additional candies as desired.

"BIRTHDAY-SAURUS" BASH CAKE

STENCIL DESIGNS

Stencils can be cut from lightweight cardboard, waxed paper or sheets of plastic cut to the size of the cake. Or, use doilies or purchased stencils. Place stencil on unfrosted, frosted or glazed cake. (Allow frostings and glazes to set before stenciling.) Sift cocoa, powdered sugar, ground cinnamon or nutmeg, colored sugars or gelatin over stencil. Carefully remove stencil to show design. For more intricate designs, use 2 or 3 different colored ingredients. (See photo of Flower Silhouette Birthday Cake on page 99.)

FLOWER SILHOUETTE BIRTHDAY CAKE

WOULDN'T THIS cake be wonderful for Mother's Day? Make your own stencil using light-weight cardboard or purchase a stencil at a craft store or paint and wallpapering store. Do not freeze the frosted cake after decorating with colored sugars, because the colors will run.

Marble Cake (page 149)
Creamy Vanilla Frosting (page 151)
Assorted colored sugars
Food color
Flower design stencil (page 97)

BAKE Marble Cake as directed for two 8- or 9-inch rounds. Prepare Creamy Vanilla Frosting; reserve $1/4$ cup. Fill layers with about $1/3$ cup remaining frosting; frost cake.

POSITION paper stencil with a flower design on top of cake. Sprinkle colored sugars over stencil, being careful not to mix colors or get sugar on other areas of cake surface; remove stencil. Tint reserved $1/4$ cup frosting with 2 drops of desired food color. Place frosting in decorating bag with writing tip #4. Pipe desired message on cake. Pipe design on edge of plate if desired.

TIME-SAVER TIP: Substitute 1 package (1 lb 2.25 oz) fudge marble cake mix with pudding for the Marble Cake. Prepare and bake as directed on package. Substitute $1^1/2$ tubs (1 lb each) vanilla ready-to-spread frosting for the Creamy Vanilla Frosting.

HAPPY BIRTHDAY CAKE

ANY COLOR can be used to decorate this versatile cake. For a more elegant cake, use Creamy Chocolate Frosting (page 151) and substitute chocolate and caramel candies for the fruit candies.

Orange-Coconut Cake (page 150)
Creamy Citrus Frosting (page 151)
Yellow food color
15 to 20 square candy fruit chews

BAKE Orange-Coconut Cake as directed for two 8- or 9-inch rounds. Prepare Creamy Citrus Frosting, using orange juice and peel. Tint $1^1/2$ cups frosting with 3 drops food color. Fill layers and frost cake with remaining frosting.

PLACE yellow frosting in decorating bag with star tip #32. Pipe shell border around top and base of cake. Pipe a ribbon and bow on each candy square to resemble a wrapped package with writing tip #4. Arrange packages on top of cake.

TIME-SAVER TIP: Substitute 1 package (1 lb 2.25 oz) yellow cake mix with pudding for the Orange-Coconut Cake. Prepare and bake as directed on package. Substitute $1^1/2$ tubs (1 lb each) vanilla ready-to-spread frosting for the Creamy Citrus Frosting.

Applesauce Cake (page 145)

3 cups plus 2 tablespoons powdered sugar

$^1/_4$ cup milk

3 tablespoons shortening

$^1/_2$ teaspoon vanilla

4 teaspoons cocoa

1 red candy-coated chocolate candy

1 round vanilla wafer cookie, about 1$^1/_2$ inches in diameter

Yellow, red and green food colors

Creamy White Frosting (page 151)

4 teaspoons cocoa

BAKE Applesauce Cake as directed for 9-inch round and 6 × 3-inch ovenproof bowl. Beat powdered sugar, milk, shortening and vanilla on medium speed until smooth. Mix 4 teaspoons cocoa into $^1/_2$ cup frosting. Reserve remaining frosting. Place cocoa frosting in decorating bag with writing tip #2. Pipe a line down center of red candy; pipe 2 small dots on each side of line to make ladybug body. Pipe a line perpendicular to the center line at one end for ladybug head; set aside.

TRACE around vanilla cookie on waxed paper with a toothpick; reserve. Pipe small dots with cocoa frosting and writing tip #4 close together on cookie to cover for center of sunflower. Tint $^1/_2$ cup of the reserved white frosting with 5 drops yellow food color and 1 drop red food color. Pipe a row of sunflower petals with yellow frosting and petal tip #352 around the traced circle on waxed paper, making sure to start petals on edge of circle. Repeat, staggering second row of petals inside circle and overlapping outer row. Place cookie sunflower center in center of petals on waxed paper. Set aside to dry.

PREPARE Creamy White Frosting; reserve $^1/_4$ cup. Tint remaining tan with 4 teaspoons cocoa and 10 drops yellow food color. Place cake layer on cake plate. Frost side with tan frosting; frost top with thin layer. Trim top of bowl cake to make flat if necessary. Place upside down in center of layer. Frost with thin layer tan frosting. Place $^2/_3$ cup tan frosting at a time in decorating bag with ribbon tip #47. Pipe a line of frosting from base of the dome, up and over to the base on the other side, dividing cake in half. Starting at the center top on either side of the piped line, continue making lines from the top to the base until there are 16 "spokes." Starting about 1 inch from top of cake, pipe over every other spoke, alternating rows to achieve a woven look.

ON the brim, at the dome base, pipe a spoke out to the cake edge in the shape of a backwards J. Repeat making an even number of spokes. Starting again at the dome base, pipe over every other spoke, working out to the cake edge.

PLACE $^1/_2$ cup of the white frosting in a decorating bag with petal tip #104. Pipe strip of frosting around base of the dome for hatband. Repeat for a second layer. Pipe about 1 tablespoon white frosting on hatband where sunflower is to be placed. Carefully remove sunflower from waxed paper; place on hatband.

MIX remaining reserved white frosting and 3 drops green food color. Pipe leaves around sunflower with green frosting and leaf tip #352, starting under petals when possible. Pipe 3 white flowers on leaves with petal tip #190. Place ladybug on a leaf. Pipe centers on white flowers with yellow frosting and writing tip #4.

PIPING BRIM OF HAT

On the brim, starting at the dome base, pipe a spoke out to the cake edge, making a backwards J.

Starting at dome base, pipe over every other spoke, working out to cake edge.

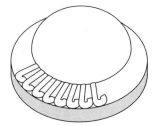

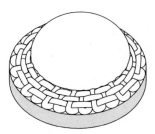

DON'T STOP at Father's Day; this cake would be great for Dad's birthday, too! Or change the message and use for any sports enthusiast.

TIME-SAVER TIP: Substitute 1 package (1 lb 2.25 oz) white cake mix with pudding for the Hazelnut Cake. Prepare and bake as directed on package. Substitute 2 tubs (1 lb each) vanilla ready-to-spread frosting for the Creamy White Frosting.

Hazelnut Cake (page 149)
Creamy White Frosting (page 151)
1 tablespoon cocoa

Tray or cardboard, 16 × 14 inches, covered
Yellow sugar

BAKE Hazelnut Cake as directed for 13 × 9-inch rectangle. Cut cake as shown in diagram. Freeze cut pieces uncovered about 1 hour for easier frosting if desired. Prepare Creamy White Frosting; reserve 1 cup. Stir cocoa into $1/2$ cup of frosting; reserve.

ARRANGE cake pieces on tray to form T-shirt as shown in diagram. Frost with white frosting, attaching sleeve with small amount of frosting. Trace lettering pattern on waxed paper. Place on top of cake and poke small holes about $1/4$ inch apart on tracing lines to outline lettering. Remove waxed paper. Place cocoa frosting in decorating bag with writing tip #4. Pipe over outline of lettering. Pipe stitching lines for sleeves, hem and neck ribbing. Fill in lettering with yellow sugar. Place reserved 1 cup white frosting in decorating bag with star tip #32. Pipe shell border around base of cake; sprinkle with yellow sugar.

CUTTING AND ASSEMBLING FATHER'S DAY T-SHIRT CAKE

Cut cake to form shirt and sleeves.

Place piece 2 on right side of cake to form shirt.

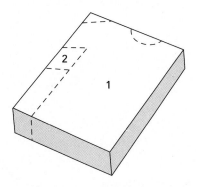

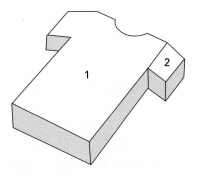

PIPING SCRIPT

Trace this pattern.

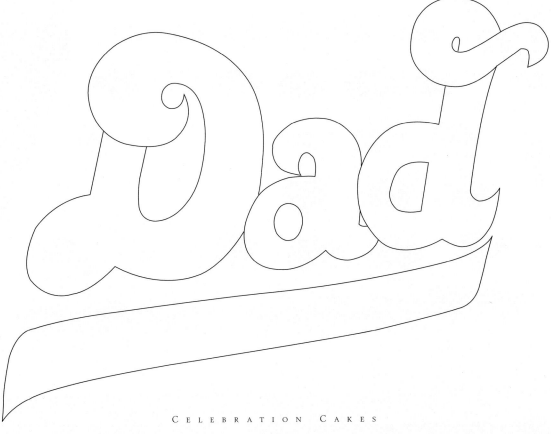

2 recipes Applesauce Cake
    (page 145)
Creamy Vanilla Frosting
    (page 151)
Tray or cardboard, 19 × 14 inches,
    covered

Blue food color
Red and black shoestring licorice
39 whole almonds
Chocolate chips

CELEBRATE A graduation, new job, promotion or birthday in the computer age!

BAKE 2 recipes Applesauce Cake as directed for 13 × 9-inch rectangle. Cut cake as shown in diagram. Freeze pieces uncovered about 1 hour for easier frosting if desired. Prepare Creamy Vanilla Frosting; reserve 3/4 cup. Arrange cake pieces on tray to form computer as shown in diagram. Frost cake, attaching pieces with small amount of frosting.

DROP 1 drop food color about 3 inches in from each corner of the screen area. Blend into frosting with spatula to within 1 inch of edges to make screen. Outline with licorice. Arrange almonds on keyboard in 5 rows of 6 and a bottom row of 9. Trim mouse to desired shape. Frost with 1/2 cup of reserved frosting. Place mouse on keyboard; attach to computer with licorice. Outline mouse key with toothpick or use a piece of white chocolate. Place remaining frosting in decorating bag with writing tip #4. Write desired message on screen. Decorate screen with chocolate chips.

TIME-SAVER TIP: Substitute 2 packages (1 lb 2.25 oz) yellow cake mix with pudding for the Applesauce Cake. Prepare and bake as directed on package. Substitute 1 1/2 tubs (1 lb each) vanilla ready-to-spread frosting for the Creamy Vanilla Frosting.

CUTTING AND ASSEMBLING COMPUTER CAKE

Cut diagonal pieces from both sides of one cake layer; cut mouse.

Arrange uncut cake layer above cut cake to form keyboard and screen. Place mouse on keyboard.

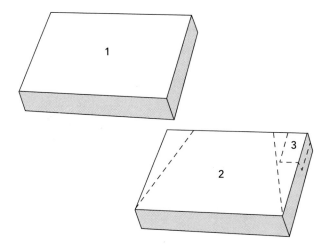

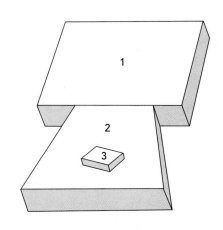

GONE FISHIN' CAKE

Buttermilk Spice Cake (page 146)
Tray or cardboard, 18 × 13 inches, covered
Creamy Vanilla Frosting (page 151)
Blue food color
1/4 cup cocoa
1 striped candy stick (5 inches)
1 ring-shaped hard candy
1 gummy frog or fish-shaped candy
3 to 5 gummy fish candies

BAKE Buttermilk Spice Cake as directed for 15 1/2 × 10 1/2 × 1-inch jelly roll. Place on tray. Prepare Creamy Vanilla Frosting. Reserve 2/3 cup for decorating. Frost cake with remaining frosting, making top smooth. Place 1 drop food color on tip of spatula. Pat color in several places along bottom of cake; swirl into frosting for water.

SIFT cocoa over reserved frosting; stir until smooth, adding 1 to 2 teaspoons water if necessary. Place cocoa frosting in decorating bag with writing tip #2. Write desired "gone fishing" message on cake. Place candy stick and ring-shaped hard candy on top of cake to form fishing rod and reel. Pipe on fishing line with cocoa frosting. Place gummy frog or gummy fish at end of fishing line for bait.

PIPE stringer on cake with cocoa frosting. Arrange gummy fish around stringer. Pipe shell border around top edge and base of cake with cocoa frosting and star tip #18.

TIME-SAVER TIP: Substitute 1 package (1 lb 2.25 oz) yellow or spice cake mix with pudding for the Buttermilk Spice Cake. Prepare and bake as directed on package.

HOUSEWARMING CAKE

Whole Wheat Applesauce Cake (page 145)
Tray or cardboard, 16 × 12 inches, covered
Creamy Vanilla Frosting (page 151)
Black shoestring licorice
Vanilla wafer cookies
Green candy sprinkles
Yellow candy fruit slice
3 cylinder licorice candies
1/2 large orange gumdrop
Green rock candy
Yellow food color
1 tube (.68 ounce) black chocolate decorating gel

BAKE Whole Wheat Applesauce Cake as directed for 13 × 9-inch rectangle. Place on tray. Prepare Creamy Vanilla Frosting; reserve 2 tablespoons. Frost cake with remaining frosting. Outline door and make bricks with a toothpick or knife.

OUTLINE door frame with shoestring licorice. Attach wafers at base of door for stoop. Use green sprinkles for grass, fruit slice for window, licorice cylinders for hinges and door handle, gumdrop for planter and rock candy for plant. Add flowers as desired.

TINT reserved frosting with 5 drops of food color. Place in decorating bag with writing tip #4. Pipe on house number and mailbox. Write new neighbor's name with decorating gel.

TIME-SAVER TIP: Substitute 1 package (1 lb 2.25 oz) yellow or spice cake mix with pudding for the Whole Wheat Applesauce Cake. Prepare and bake as directed on package.

BAR AND Bat Mitzvahs, a trip to Israel and Hebrew school parties are all wonderful occasions for this cake.

TIME-SAVER TIP: Substitute 1 package (1 lb 2.25 oz) white cake mix with pudding for the White Cake. Prepare and bake as directed on package. Substitute 2 tubs (1 lb each) vanilla ready-to-spread frosting for the Creamy White Frosting.

White Cake (page 149)
Creamy White Frosting (page 151)
Tray or cardboard, 14 × 14 inches, covered

Food color
Colored sugar

BAKE White Cake as directed for 13 × 9-inch rectangle. Cut cake as shown in diagram. Freeze cut pieces uncovered about 1 hour for easier frosting if desired. Prepare Creamy White Frosting; reserve 1 1/2 cups.

ARRANGE cake pieces on tray to form star as shown in diagram, attaching pieces with small amount of frosting. Frost cake with remaining white frosting. Place 1/2 cup of the reserved frosting in decorating bag with star tip #32. Pipe shell border around base of cake. Tint remaining reserved frosting with desired food color. Pipe 3 rows of stars with star tip #32 around top edge of cake, starting and stopping so that triangles appear interwoven. Sprinkle frosting top of cake lightly with sugar; sprinkle on border if desired.

CUTTING AND ASSEMBLING STAR OF DAVID CAKE

Cut cake to form one large triangle and three smaller ones.

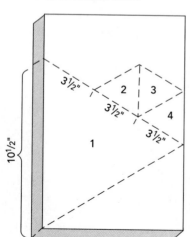

Arrange smaller triangles around large triangle to complete star points.

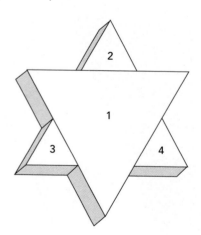

STAR OF DAVID CAKE

FOUR

Specialty Bakery Cakes

Custard-Filled Nutmeg Cake *112*

French Silk Filbert Cake *113*

Caramel-Pecan Torte *114*

Chocolate Cookie Cake *116*

Decadent Chocolate Cake *117*

Maple-Pecan Cake *118*

Strawberries and Cream Cake *119*

Lemon Meringue Cake *120*

Mocha Cream Torte *122*

Walnut Torte *122*

Marzipan Torte *126*

Chocolate Mint Loaves *128*

Custard-Filled Nutmeg Cake (page 112) and French Silk Filbert Cake (page 113)

CUSTARD-FILLED NUTMEG CAKE

Nutmeg Cake (below)
Custard Cream Filling (right)
Powdered sugar
Stencil or paper doily
Fresh berries
Mint leaves

BAKE Nutmeg Cake as directed. Prepare Custard Cream Filling. Split cake horizontally to make 4 layers (see Splitting Cake Layer on page 132). Spread each of 3 layers with one-third of the filling. Place remaining layer on top. Place stencil on top layer; press powdered sugar generously through sieve over stencil. Carefully remove stencil. Apply second layer of stenciling using ground nutmeg if desired. Garnish base of cake with berries and mint leaves. Refrigerate any remaining cake. *16 servings.*

NUTMEG CAKE

2 cups plus 2 tablespoons all-purpose flour
1 1/2 cups sugar
1/2 cup shortening
1 cup milk
3 1/2 teaspoons baking powder
1 teaspoon salt
1 teaspoon ground nutmeg
1 teaspoon vanilla
3 eggs

HEAT oven to 350°. Grease and flour 2 round pans, 9 × 1 1/2 inches. Beat all ingredients in large bowl on medium speed 30 seconds, scraping bowl constantly. Beat on high speed 3 minutes, scraping bowl occasionally. Pour batter into pans.

BAKE 30 to 35 minutes or until toothpick inserted in center comes out clean. Cool 10 minutes; remove from pans. Cool completely.

CUSTARD CREAM FILLING

2/3 cup sugar
4 tablespoons cornstarch
1/4 teaspoon salt
3 cups milk
4 egg yolks, slightly beaten
1 1/2 teaspoons vanilla

MIX sugar, cornstarch and salt in 2-quart saucepan. Stir in milk gradually. Cook over medium heat, stirring constantly, until mixture thickens and boils. Boil and stir 1 minute. Stir about half of the hot mixture gradually into egg yolks. Blend into hot mixture in saucepan. Boil and stir 1 minute; remove from heat. Stir in vanilla; cool.

TIME-SAVER TIP: Substitute 1 package (1 lb 2.25 oz) yellow cake mix with pudding for the Nutmeg Cake. Prepare and bake as directed on package—except add 1 teaspoon ground nutmeg before beating.

White Nut Cake (below)
French Silk Frosting (right)
*12 whole hazelnuts**
*1 cup finely chopped hazelnuts**

BAKE White Nut Cake as directed. Reserve $^1/_2$ cup French Silk Frosting for decorating; fill layers and frost cake with remaining frosting. Mark servings on frosting with serrated knife.

PLACE reserved frosting in decorating bag with star tip #18. Pipe three-petaled lily onto each serving. Place 1 whole filbert on each lily. Press chopped hazelnuts into frosting around side. *12 servings.*

WHITE NUT CAKE

6 egg whites
$^1/_4$ cup sugar
$2^2/_3$ cups all-purpose flour
*$1^1/_2$ cups finely chopped hazelnuts**
$1^1/_4$ cups sugar
$^1/_2$ cup (1 stick) margarine or butter, softened
$^1/_2$ cup shortening
4 teaspoons baking powder
1 teaspoon salt
1 cup milk

HEAT oven to 350°. Grease and flour 3 round pans, 8 × $1^1/_2$ inches. Beat egg whites in large bowl until foamy. Beat in $^1/_4$ cup sugar, 1 tablespoon at a time; continue beating until stiff and glossy. Do not underbeat.

BEAT flour, hazelnuts, $1^1/_4$ cups sugar, the margarine, shortening, baking powder and salt in another large bowl on medium speed 30 seconds, scraping bowl constantly. Beat in milk on medium speed 2 minutes, scraping bowl occasionally; fold into egg whites. Pour batter into pans.

BAKE 35 to 40 minutes or until toothpick inserted in center comes out clean. (Refrigerate 1 layer while 2 are baking.) Cool 10 minutes, remove from pans. Cool completely.

FRENCH SILK FROSTING

4 cups powdered sugar
1 cup (2 sticks) margarine or butter, softened
3 tablespoons milk
$1^1/_2$ teaspoons vanilla
3 ounces unsweetened chocolate, melted and cooled

BEAT all ingredients on medium speed until frosting is smooth and of spreading consistency. If necessary, stir in additional milk, 1 teaspoon at a time.

TIME-SAVER TIP: Substitute 1 package (1 lb 2.25 oz) white cake mix with pudding for the White Nut Cake. Prepare and bake as directed on package for two 8-inch rounds—except stir $^1/_2$ cup finely chopped hazelnuts into batter.

*Finely chopped pecans can be substituted for the finely chopped hazelnuts in the cake batter and around the frosted cake. Substitute pecan halves for the whole hazelnuts on top of the frosted cake.

CARAMEL-PECAN TORTE

Caramel Cake (below)
Caramel Frosting (right)
1 to 2 teaspoons milk
Chopped pecans or Chocolate-Dipped Nuts (below)

BAKE Caramel Cake as directed. Cut cake horizontally into 3 layers. Reserve $^1/_2$ cup Caramel Frosting. Fill layers with remaining frosting. Stir milk into reserved frosting until of drizzling consistency; drizzle over cake. Garnish with chopped pecans. *18 servings.*

CARAMEL CAKE

$2^1/_4$ cups all-purpose flour
$1^3/_4$ cups packed brown sugar
$^1/_2$ cup shortening
1 cup milk
3 teaspoons baking powder
$^1/_2$ teaspoon salt
1 teaspoon vanilla
2 eggs
$^1/_2$ cup chopped pecans

HEAT oven to 350°. Grease and flour 12-cup bundt cake pan. Beat all ingredients except pecans in large bowl on low speed 30 seconds, scraping bowl constantly. Beat on high speed 3 minutes, scraping bowl frequently. Stir in pecans. Pour batter into pan.

BAKE 35 to 40 minutes or until toothpick inserted in center comes out clean. Cool 20 minutes; invert onto wire rack. Cool completely.

CARAMEL FROSTING

$^1/_2$ cup (1 stick) margarine or butter
1 cup packed brown sugar
$^1/_4$ cup milk
2 cups powdered sugar

HEAT margarine over medium heat in 2-quart saucepan until melted. Stir in brown sugar. Heat to boiling, stirring constantly. Reduce heat to low. Boil and stir 2 minutes. Stir in milk. Heat to boiling; remove from heat. Cool to lukewarm. Gradually stir in powdered sugar. Place saucepan of frosting in bowl of cold water. Beat until smooth and of spreading consistency. If frosting becomes too stiff, stir in additional milk, 1 teaspoon at a time.

CHOCOLATE-DIPPED NUTS OR FRUITS

Melt $1^1/_2$ ounces bittersweet chocolate, chopped and 2 teaspoons shortening. Coat 12 whole nut halves or pieces of dried fruit $^3/_4$ of the way; place on waxed-paper lined cookie sheet. Refrigerate uncovered until chocolate is firm, at least 30 minutes but no longer than 24 hours. See page 143 for Chocolate Tips.

CHOCOLATE COOKIE CAKE (PAGE 116) AND CARAMEL-PECAN TORTE

WHEN YOU need a smaller cake, just cut the recipe in half and bake it in one layer.

Cookie-Sour Cream Cake (below)
3/4 cup whipping (heavy) cream
1 tablespoon sugar
3 creme-filled sandwich cookies, cut in half
Chocolate cookie crumbs

BAKE Cookie-Sour Cream Cake, as directed. Beat whipping cream and sugar in chilled bowl until stiff. Place 1 cake layer on serving plate; spread with half of the whipped cream. Repeat with remaining layer and whipped cream. Garnish with cookie halves and cookie crumbs. *16 servings.*

COOKIE-SOUR CREAM CAKE

2 cups all-purpose flour
1 1/2 cups sugar
1 cup sour cream
1/2 cup (1 stick) margarine or butter, softened
1/2 cup water
1 teaspoon baking soda
1 teaspoon baking powder
2 eggs
16 creme-filled sandwich cookies, coarsely chopped

HEAT oven to 350°. Grease and flour 2 round pans, 8 × 1 1/2 or 9 × 1 1/2 inches. Beat all ingredients except cookies in large bowl on low speed 30 seconds, scraping bowl constantly. Beat on high speed 2 minutes, scraping bowl occasionally . Stir in cookies. Pour into pans.

BAKE 30 to 35 minutes or until cake springs back when touched lightly in center. Cool 10 minutes; remove from pans. Cool completely.

DECADENT CHOCOLATE CAKE AND MAPLE-PECAN CAKE (PAGE 118)

DECADENT CHOCOLATE CAKE

1 cup semisweet chocolate chips
$^{1}/_{2}$ cup (1 stick) margarine or
    butter
$^{1}/_{2}$ cup all-purpose flour or cake
    flour
4 eggs, separated
$^{1}/_{2}$ cup sugar

$^{1}/_{2}$ cup semisweet chocolate chips
2 tablespoons margarine or butter
2 tablespoons light corn syrup
Raspberry Sauce (below)
$^{1}/_{2}$ cup whipped cream

IF YOU know that you will be serving the whole cake at once, pipe 12 whipped cream rosettes on the cake, one on each serving, and pile a few raspberries in the center just before serving. It'll be a showstopper!

HEAT oven to 325°. Grease springform pan, 8 × 2$^{1}/_{2}$ inches, or round pan, 9 × 1$^{1}/_{2}$ inches. Heat 1 cup chocolate chips and $^{1}/_{2}$ cup margarine in 2-quart heavy saucepan over medium heat until chocolate chips are melted; cool 5 minutes. Stir in flour until smooth. Stir in egg yolks until well blended.

BEAT egg whites in large bowl on high speed until foamy. Beat in sugar, 1 tablespoon at a time, until soft peaks form. Fold chocolate mixture into egg whites. Spread batter in pan.

BAKE springform 35 to 40 minutes, round 30 to 35 minutes (top will appear dry and cracked) or until toothpick inserted in center comes out clean; cool 10 minutes. Run knife along side of cake to loosen; remove side of springform pan. Invert cake onto wire rack; remove bottom of springform pan. Cool completely. Place on serving plate.

HEAT $^{1}/_{2}$ cup chocolate chips, 2 tablespoons margarine and the corn syrup over medium heat until chocolate chips are melted. Spread over top of cake, allowing some to drizzle down side. Place whipped cream in decorating bag. Pipe a rosette on each serving; sprinkle with cocoa if desired. Serve with Raspberry Sauce. Garnish with fresh strawberries if desired. *12 servings.*

RASPBERRY SAUCE

1 package (10 ounces) frozen raspberries, thawed, drained and juice
    reserved
$^{1}/_{4}$ cup sugar
2 tablespoons cornstarch
1 to 2 tablespoons orange- or raspberry-flavored liqueur, if desired

ADD enough water to reserved juice to measure 1 cup. Mix sugar and cornstarch in 1-quart saucepan. Stir in juice and raspberries. Heat to boiling over medium heat. Boil and stir 1 minute; strain. Stir in liqueur.

Maple-Buttermilk Cake (below)
Maple-Butter Frosting (right)
1 cup finely chopped pecans
Chocolate Twigs (page 144), if desired
Malted-milk balls, if desired

BAKE Maple-Buttermilk Cake as directed. Fill layers and frost side only with Maple-Butter Frosting. Place pecans on waxed paper. Hold cake as shown in diagram; roll side carefully in pecans to coat. Frost top of cake with remaining frosting in spiral design using large spatula. Garnish with Chocolate Twigs and malted-milk balls. *14 to 16 servings.*

M A P L E - B U T T E R M I L K   C A K E

2¹/₂ cups all-purpose flour or 1²/₃ cups cake flour
1¹/₂ cups sugar
¹/₂ cup (1 stick) margarine or butter, softened
¹/₄ cup shortening
1¹/₂ cups buttermilk
1¹/₂ teaspoons baking soda
³/₄ teaspoon salt
1¹/₂ teaspoons maple flavoring
3 eggs

HEAT oven to 350°. Grease and flour 2 round pans, 9 × 1¹/₂ inches, or 3 round pans, 8 × 1¹/₂ inches. Beat all ingredients in large bowl on medium speed 30 seconds, scraping bowl constantly. Beat on high speed 3 minutes, scraping bowl occasionally. Pour batter into pans.

BAKE 30 to 35 minutes or until toothpick inserted in center comes out clean. Cool 10 minutes; remove from pans. Cool completely.

M A P L E - B U T T E R   F R O S T I N G

3 cups powdered sugar
¹/₃ cup margarine or butter, softened
¹/₃ cup maple-flavored syrup

MIX all ingredients. Beat until frosting is smooth and of spreading consistency. If necessary, stir in additional syrup, ¹/₂ teaspoon at a time.

C O A T I N G   S I D E S   O F   C A K E S

Two filled cake layers can be rolled in chopped nuts, candies or flaked or shredded coconut to coat sides. Frost side of cake only. Place nuts on waxed paper. Hold cake as shown and roll carefully in nuts to coat. Frost top of cake. (See photo of Maple-Pecan Cake on page 116.)

DO YOU love raspberries or peaches? Any berries or cut-up fruit can be substituted for the strawberries in this luscious cake.

Whipped Cream Cake (below)
Whipped Cream Cheese Frosting (right)
1 pint strawberries, sliced
Mint leaves, if desired

BAKE Whipped Cream Cake as directed. Spread 1 layer with $1/2$ cup of the Whipped Cream Cheese Frosting; top with layer of sliced strawberries. Place remaining cake layer on top. Spread thin layer of frosting on side of cake.

PLACE remaining frosting in decorating bag with large open star tip #4B. Pipe vertical rows on side of cake. Pipe shell border around top edge of cake. Arrange remaining sliced strawberries on top of cake. Garnish with mint leaves. Refrigerate remaining cake. *16 servings.*

WHIPPED CREAM CAKE

2 cups all-purpose flour or $2^1/4$ cups cake flour
$1^1/2$ cups sugar
2 teaspoons baking powder
$1/2$ teaspoon salt
$1^1/2$ cups whipping (heavy) cream
3 eggs
$1^1/2$ teaspoons vanilla

HEAT oven to 350°. Grease and flour 2 round pans, 8 × $1^1/2$ or 9 × $1^1/2$ inches. Mix flour, sugar, baking powder and salt. Beat whipping cream in chilled large bowl until stiff. Beat eggs in small bowl about 5 minutes or until very thick and lemon colored. Fold eggs and vanilla into whipped cream. Add flour mixture, about $1/2$ cup at a time, folding gently after each addition until blended. Pour batter into pans.

BAKE 30 to 35 minutes or until toothpick inserted in center comes out clean. Cool 10 minutes; remove from pans. Cool completely.

WHIPPED CREAM CHEESE FROSTING

1 package (3 ounces) cream cheese, softened
1 tablespoon milk
2 cups whipping (heavy) cream
$2/3$ cup powdered sugar

BEAT cream cheese and milk in chilled bowl on low speed until smooth; beat in whipping cream and powdered sugar. Beat on high speed, scraping bowl occasionally, until stiff peaks form.

TIME-SAVER TIP: Substitute 1 package (1 lb 2.25 oz) yellow cake mix with pudding for the Whipped Cream Cake. Prepare and bake as directed on package.

LEMON MERINGUE CAKE

Meringue Cake (below)

1 package (4-serving size) lemon
 pudding and pie filling (not
 instant)

$^1/_2$ cup whipped cream

Lemon wedges if desired

BAKE Meringue Cake as directed. Prepare pudding and pie filling as directed on package. Refrigerate about $1^1/_2$ hours or until chilled. Stir pudding; spread $1^1/_4$ cups over meringue on 1 cake layer. Place remaining layer, meringue side up, on pudding. Spread with remaining pudding. Place whipped cream in decorating bag with star tip. Pipe on whipped cream, or garnish with whipped cream as desired. Garnish with lemon wedges. Serve within 30 minutes. Refrigerate remaining cake. *8 to 10 servings.*

MERINGUE CAKE

$1^1/_2$ cups cake flour

$^3/_4$ cup sugar

$1^1/_2$ teaspoons baking powder

$^1/_2$ teaspoon salt

$^3/_4$ cup shortening

$^2/_3$ cup milk

$1^1/_2$ teaspoons vanilla

4 eggs, separated

1 cup sugar

HEAT oven to 325°. Grease sides of 2 round pans, 9 × $1^1/_2$ or 8 × $1^1/_2$ inches. Line bottoms of pans with cooking parchment paper or waxed paper circles. Beat flour, $^3/_4$ cup sugar, the baking powder, salt, shortening, milk, vanilla and egg yolks in medium bowl on low speed 30 seconds, scraping bowl constantly. Beat on high speed 2 minutes, scraping bowl occasionally (batter will be stiff). Spread evenly in pans.

BEAT egg whites in small bowl on medium speed until foamy. Beat in 1 cup sugar, 1 tablespoon at a time, on high speed until stiff peaks form. Spread half of the egg white mixture over batter in each pan.

BAKE 30 to 35 minutes or until meringue looks set and dry. Cool 10 minutes. Loosen meringues from edges of pans with knife point if necessary. Carefully remove from pans and peel off paper. Place layers, meringue sides up, on wire racks. Cool completely.

FRESH FRUIT DECORATIONS

Fresh Fruit   A great variety of fresh fruits are now available. Choose fruits at their seasonal peak for the fullest flavors and the most economical prices. Choose ripe, but firm, fruits that will hold their shapes.

Whole raspberries, blueberries or blackberries, whole and sliced strawberries, sliced kiwifruit, starfruit or papaya and orange segments are good choices because they do not turn brown. If using sliced peaches, nectarines, apples, bananas or mangos, dip fruit in water mixed with lemon juice; drain well. Place fruits on cake just before serving. Refrigerate any remaining cake.

Frosted Grapes   Dip small clusters of grapes into water, then into superfine or granulated sugar. Dry clusters on wire rack before adding to cake. Champagne grapes are especially attractive this way. Whole cranberries can also be frosted.

M O C H A   C R E A M   T O R T E

Golden Pound Cake (page 126)
Mocha Cream Frosting (below)
Chocolate Curls (page 144)
Chocolate coffee beans

PREPARE Golden Pound Cake as directed—except grease and flour loaf pan, 9 × 5 × 3 inches, omit almond extract and increase bake time to 60 to 65 minutes. Freeze cooled cake uncovered about $1^1/2$ hours or until firm. Cut cake horizontally into 5 layers. Spread scant $1/4$ cup Mocha Cream Frosting between each layer, frost sides and top of cake with remaining frosting.

MARK diagonal lines with tines of fork across top and down sides of cake. Garnish with Chocolate Curls made with white chocolate and chocolate coffee beans. 16 servings.

M O C H A   C R E A M   F R O S T I N G

1 tablespoon instant coffee
2 tablespoons hot water
4 cups powdered sugar
$3/4$ cup margarine or butter, softened
1 tablespoon cocoa
1 teaspoon water

DISSOLVE instant coffee in the hot water. Beat coffee and remaining ingredients on medium speed until smooth and of spreading consistency. If necessary, stir in additional water, $1/2$ teaspoon at a time.

TIME-SAVER TIP: Substitute 1 package (1 lb) pound cake mix for the Pound Cake. Prepare and bake as directed on package.

W A L N U T   T O R T E

$1^1/2$ cups chopped walnuts
$1^1/2$ cups vanilla wafer crumbs
1 cup packed brown sugar
1 cup (2 sticks) margarine or butter, melted
Dark Cocoa Cake (page 147)
$1^1/2$ cups whipping (heavy) cream
3 tablespoons granulated sugar
1 teaspoon vanilla
Chocolate Leaves (page 78), if desired

HEAT oven to 350°. Line 2 ungreased round pans, 9 × $1^1/2$ inches, with cooking parchment paper or waxed paper circles. Mix walnuts, wafer crumbs, brown sugar and margarine. Spread about $3/4$ cup mixture in each pan; reserve remaining walnut mixture. Prepare Dark Cocoa Cake as directed. Pour about $1^1/2$ cups batter over walnut mixture in each pan; refrigerate remaining batter.

BAKE about 20 minutes or until top springs back when touched lightly. Immediately remove from pans; invert. Repeat with remaining walnut mixture and batter. Cool layers completely.

BEAT whipping cream, granulated sugar and vanilla in chilled small bowl until stiff. Place 1 cake layer, walnut side up, on serving plate; spread with about $3/4$ cup whipped cream. Repeat with remaining layers and whipped cream. Or, place whipped cream for top layer in decorating bag with star tip #6. Pipe rosettes in center of cake and garnish with Chocolate Leaves. Refrigerate any remaining cake. 16 servings.

TIME-SAVER TIP: Substitute 1 package (1 lb 2.25 oz) devil's food cake mix with pudding for the Dark Cocoa Cake. Prepare batter as directed on package. Continue as directed above.

WALNUT TORTE AND MOCHA CREAM TORTE

GLAZED WHOLE WHEAT FRUITCAKE

1¹/₂ cups whole wheat flour
1¹/₂ cups all-purpose flour
1¹/₄ cups sugar
³/₄ cup margarine or butter, softened
³/₄ cup shortening
²/₃ cup orange juice
1¹/₂ teaspoons baking powder
³/₄ teaspoon salt
9 eggs
1 lb candied cherries, cut into halves (about 2¹/₂ cups)
15 ounces golden raisins (about 3 cups)
12 ounces candied pineapple, cut up (about 2 cups)
4 ounces candied citron, cut up (about ²/₃ cup)
4 ounces candied orange peel, cut up (about ²/₃ cup)
³/₄ cup flaked coconut
8 ounces blanched whole almonds (about 1¹/₂ cups)
8 ounces pecan halves (about 2 cups)
¹/₄ cup apple jelly, melted

HEAT oven to 275°. Line 2 loaf pans, 9 × 5 × 3 inches, with aluminum foil; grease. Beat flours, sugar, margarine, shortening, orange juice, baking powder, salt and eggs in large bowl on medium speed, scraping bowl constantly, until blended, about 30 seconds. Beat on high speed, scraping bowl occasionally, 3 minutes. Mix batter into fruits and nuts in 6-quart bowl. Spread mixture in pans.

BAKE 2¹/₂ to 3 hours or until wooden pick inserted in center comes out clean. Remove from pans; cool.

SPREAD with melted apple jelly and decorate with blanched almonds or candied fruit, if desired. *2 loaves.*

FRUITCAKE RING

Mincemeat Fruitcake (below)
Browned Butter Glaze (below)
¹/₃ cup coarsely chopped pecans

BAKE Mincemeat Fruitcake as directed. Spread with Browned Butter Glaze, letting it run down side unevenly. Immediately sprinkle top with pecans.

MINCEMEAT FRUITCAKE

2 eggs
1 jar (28 ounces) ready-to-use mincemeat
1 lb mixed candied fruit (about 2 cups)
1 can (14 ounces) sweetened condensed milk
1 cup coarsely chopped pecans
2¹/₂ cups all-purpose flour
1 teaspoon baking soda

HEAT oven to 300°. Generously grease and flour 12-cup bundt cake pan or tube pan, 10 × 4 inches. Beat eggs slightly in large bowl. Stir in mincemeat, candied fruit, sweetened condensed milk and pecans. Stir in flour and baking soda. Pour batter into pan.

BAKE about 1 hour 50 minutes or until wooden pick inserted in center comes out clean. Cool 15 minutes; remove from pan. Cool completely.

BROWNED BUTTER GLAZE

2 tablespoons margarine or butter
1 cup powdered sugar
1 teaspoon vanilla
1 tablespoon hot water

HEAT margarine in saucepan over medium heat until delicate brown. Cool slightly. Stir in powdered sugar, vanilla and water. If necessary, stir in additional hot water, 1 teaspoon at a time, until glaze is desired consistency.

Golden Pound Cake (page 127)

1 jar (12 ounces) apricot preserves

1 package (7 ounces) marzipan

$^1/_2$ cup sliced almonds

$^1/_2$ cup powdered sugar

2 teaspoons water

2 teaspoons cocoa

Red food color

TIME-SAVER TIP: Substitute 1
package (1 lb) pound cake mix for
the Golden Pound Cake. Prepare
as directed on package—except
add 1 teaspoon almond extract
before beating. Bake in 2 round
pans, 8 X 1$^1/_2$ inches, 30 to 35
minutes.

BAKE Golden Pound Cake as directed. Split cake horizontally to make 4 layers (see page 132). If necessary, break up any large pieces of apricot in preserves. Fill each layer with scant $^1/_4$ cup of the apricot preserves. Brush side and top of cake lightly with preserves.

RESERVE half of the marzipan for top of cake. Shape half of the remaining marzipan into rectangle, about 4 × 1 inch. Roll between sheets of waxed paper into rectangle, 12 × 3 inches (marzipan will be very thin). Trim sides to make even, pressing trimmings on ends if necessary to make 12 × 3-inch rectangle.

PEEL top sheet of waxed paper off marzipan. Using bottom sheet of waxed paper to help transfer, lift marzipan and waxed paper together as shown in diagram and carefully press marzipan onto half of cake side (press any excess over top edge of cake). Remove waxed paper. Repeat with remaining fourth of marzipan. Smooth edges together with spatula to join.

ADD any remaining marzipan trimmings to reserved half of marzipan; shape into flattened round. Roll between sheets of waxed paper into 8-inch circle. Peel top sheet of waxed paper off marzipan. Lift remaining waxed paper and marzipan together, invert and press onto top of cake. Press to join marzipan around top edge of cake. Carefully remove waxed paper. Brush side only of cake lightly with apricot preserves; press almonds into marzipan to coat side of cake.

MIX powdered sugar and water; reserve 1 tablespoon for flowers. Stir cocoa and enough additional water, a few drops at a time, into remaining frosting until of spreading consistency. Place in small, sturdy plastic storage bag; cut off very small corner of bag to make writing tip. Draw desired design lightly in marzipan with toothpick. Fold over top of bag; press out frosting to follow design.

STIR 3 or 4 drops red food color into reserved frosting. Place in another small, sturdy plastic storage bag; cut off very small corner of bag to make writing tip. Pipe 3 to 5 dots to form each flower. *16 servings.*

Note   Keep marzipan covered at all times to prevent it from drying out. If marzipan sticks to hands, sprinkle hands lightly with powdered sugar. Marzipan can be rerolled easily if necessary. When rolling marzipan for side of cake, lift rolling pin slightly at ends of marzipan to prevent ends from becoming too thin. When rolling marzipan for top, roll from center to outside evenly in all directions.

GOLDEN POUND CAKE

HEAT oven to 350°. Grease and flour 2 round pans, 8 × 1¹/₂ inches. Beat all ingredients in large bowl on medium speed 30 seconds, scraping bowl constantly. Beat on high speed 3 minutes, scraping bowl occasionally. Pour batter into pans.

BAKE 30 to 35 minutes or until toothpick inserted in center comes out clean. Cool 10 minutes; remove from pans. Cool completely.

2 cups all-purpose flour

1 cup sugar

¹/₄ cup (¹/₂ stick) margarine or butter, softened

¹/₄ cup shortening

³/₄ cup milk

3 teaspoons baking powder

1 teaspoon salt

1 teaspoon almond extract

1 teaspoon vanilla

2 eggs

PLACING MARZIPAN ON MARZIPAN TORTE

Lift marzipan and waxed paper together; press marzipan onto half of cake side. Remove wax paper. Repeat with remaining side.

CHOCOLATE MINT LOAVES (PAGE 128) AND MARZIPAN TORTE

CHOCOLATE MINT LOAVES

USE HOLIDAY mints for different seasons of the year. Try orange for Halloween, for instance.

Peppermint Chiffon Cake (below)
Chocolate-Mint Frosting (right)
7 to 10 square or rectangular chocolate party mints

BAKE Peppermint Chiffon Cake as directed. Remove loaves from pans. Reserve 3 cups Chocolate-Mint Frosting for decorating; frost loaves with remaining frosting. Place reserved frosting in decorating bag with large open star tip #4B. Pipe frosting in continuous motion back and forth across tops of loaves. Cut party mints diagonally in half; decorate tops of loaves. Refrigerate any remaining cake. *16 servings.*

PEPPERMINT CHIFFON CAKE

2 cups all-purpose flour
1^1/2 cups sugar
3 teaspoons baking powder
1 teaspoon salt
^{3}/4 cup cold water
^{1}/2 cup vegetable oil
^{1}/2 teaspoon peppermint extract
7 egg yolks
1 cup egg whites (about 8)
^{1}/2 teaspoon cream of tartar

HEAT oven to 325°. Mix flour, sugar, baking powder and salt in large bowl. Beat in water, oil, peppermint extract and egg yolk with spoon until smooth.

BEAT egg whites and cream of tartar in another large bowl on medium speed until stiff peaks form. Pour egg yolk mixture gradually over beaten egg whites, folding with rubber spatula just until blended. Divide batter between 2 ungreased loaf pans, 9 × 5 × 3 inches.

BAKE 50 to 55 minutes or until top springs back when touched lightly. Invert pans with edges on 2 other pans; let hang until cakes are cold.

CHOCOLATE-MINT FROSTING

3 cups whipping (heavy) cream
1^1/2 cups powdered sugar
^{3}/4 cup cocoa
^{1}/2 teaspoon peppermint extract

BEAT all ingredients in chilled bowl until stiff.

FIVE

Cake Basics

The Basics *130*

Chocolate Tips *143*

Angel Food Cake *145*

Applesauce Cake *145*

Buttermilk Spice Cake *146*

Carrot Cake *146*

Dark Cocoa Cake *147*

Double Chocolate Cake *147*

Pound Cake *148*

Pumpkin-Gingerbread Cake *148*

White Cake *149*

Yellow Cake *150*

Buttercream Frosting *150*

Chocolate Decorator Frosting *150*

Creamy Chocolate Frosting *151*

Creamy Vanilla Frosting *151*

Creamy White Frosting *151*

Cream Cheese Frosting *151*

Easy Penuche Frosting *152*

White Decorator Frosting *152*

White Mountain Frosting *152*

Chocolate Glaze *153*

White Chocolate Glaze *153*

Petits Fours Glaze *153*

THE BASICS

The equipment, tips and techniques described here are your guide to the best and easiest ways to bake, frost and decorate your beautiful special occasion cakes. Practice will give you confidence and assure you of terrific results every time.

MEASURING INGREDIENTS

Measuring Dry Ingredients

Use graduated nested measuring cups for measuring nonliquids. For granulated sugar, dip the cup into the sugar to fill, then level with a straight-edged knife or spatula. Do not sift flour to measure or to combine with other ingredients.

For all-purpose flour, cake flour and powdered sugar, lightly spoon into cup, then level with a straight-edged knife or spatula. (Sift powdered sugar only if it is lumpy—if it is sifted the quantity may need to be increased.)

Spoon brown sugar and shortening into the cup, then pack down firmly. For nuts, coconut and cut-up or small fruit, lightly spoon into the cup, then pack down lightly.

Measuring Liquid Ingredients

Glass measuring cups are used for measuring liquids. Read the measurement at eye level.

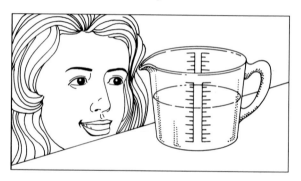

Using Measuring Spoons

Graduated measuring spoons are used to measure thin or thick liquids and dry ingredients. Pour thin liquids into the appropriate spoon until full.

For dry ingredients and thick liquids, pour or scoop into the appropriate spoon until full, then level with a straight-edged knife or spatula. If your set of spoons does not have a $^{1}/_{8}$ teaspoon measure, use the $^{1}/_{4}$ teaspoon, fill it and remove half.

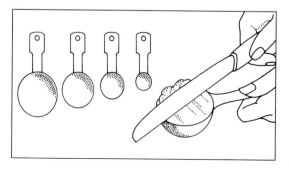

THE BASICS

EGG VOLUMES

Large Eggs	Measurement
2 eggs	$1/3$ to $1/2$ cup
3 eggs	$1/2$ to $2/3$ cup
4 eggs	$2/3$ to 1 cup
1 egg white	about 2 tablespoons
1 egg yolk	about 1 $1/2$ tablespoons

Beating Cake Batter

Surveys show that the majority of mixers in use in the United States are the portable type; our cakes have been tested with both the portable and standard electric mixer. Standard mixers are usually more powerful than portable. So, for the initial step of beating layer cake ingredients until blended, reduce the speed of the standard mixer to low to prevent splattering.

You can also mix cakes by hand. Stir the ingredients to moisten and blend them; then beat 150 strokes for every minute of beating time (3 minutes equals 450 strokes). You'll need practice before this seems easy; while you're practicing, cake volume may not be as high.

Using Eggs

Our cake recipes have been tested with large eggs. Eggs are also available in medium and extra large. If using a size other than large, use the Egg Volumes (above) for the correct equivalent.

For better volume, let egg whites stand at room temperature about 15 minutes before beating. Beat whites in a clean, dry metal bowl with a clean beater. Any yolk or fat in the whites will prevent them from beating properly.

Leftover egg whites can be stored covered in the refrigerator 7 to 10 days. Leftover egg yolks should be covered with water and can be stored in a covered container in the refrigerator 2 to 3 days. To freeze whites, place in a plastic ice cube tray, then remove the frozen cubes to a plastic freezer bag for storage. Thaw frozen whites in the refrigerator.

Leftover yolks can be used in custards, scrambled eggs, boiled dressings, egg pastries and cake fillings.

Margarine, Butter or Shortening

When our recipes call for margarine or butter, they have been tested using stick-type margarine and butter. **We do not recommend vegetable oil spreads with less than 65 percent fat be used for baking.** When they call for shortening, they have been tested with solid vegetable shortening. Unless oil is called for (as with chiffon-type cakes), never substitute oil even if the recipe calls for melted shortening, margarine or butter.

Baking Cakes

Always use the size pans called for in the recipe. To check the width of a pan, measure across the top from inside edge to inside edge. Baking a cake in too large a pan will result in a pale, flat, shrunken cake. Too small or too shallow a pan will result in a cake that bulges and loses its shape.

Shiny metal pans reflect heat away from the cake. They produce a tender, light brown crust and are preferred for baking cakes.

Dark nonstick or glass baking pans should be used by following the manufacturers' directions. These pans readily absorb heat and a better result is often achieved if the baking temperature is reduced 25°.

Cooling and Removing Angel Food and Chiffon Cakes from Pan

Invert the pan on a heatproof funnel or bottle and let hang until cake is cold.

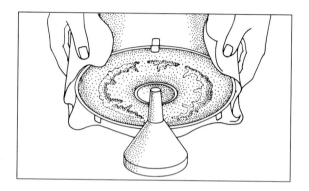

Loosen the cake by moving a spatula or table knife up and down against side of pan.

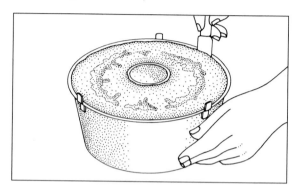

Splitting Angel Food and Chiffon Cakes into Layers

Measure the cake with a ruler and mark into equal widths the number of desired layers with wooden picks.

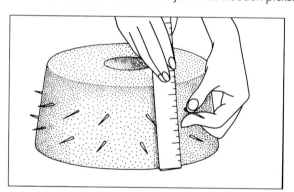

Using a serrated knife and with wooden picks as a guide, cut across the cake with a light, sawing motion.

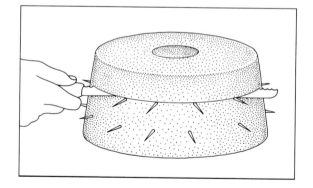

Use of Dowels

If you wish, dowels or legs can be added to large tiered cakes for support and stability. Dowels should be about $1/8$ inch higher than each tier (see illustration, page 135). Insert the dowel through tier to plate or cardboard round. Use 4 to 8 dowels per tier, depending on the size of the layer.

Arrange the dowels in a circle, square or rectangle slightly smaller than the tier placed directly on top of them. Place the next tier on cardboard round on top of the dowels. Repeat with remaining tiers except the top tier. Dowels can be of wood or plastic. If using separators or columns, refer to the manufacturer's directions.

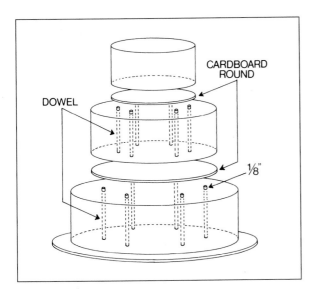

CARDBOARD ROUND

DOWEL

⅛"

Cutting and Frosting Cut-Up Cakes

Cakes may be frozen before cutting to minimize crumbling during cutting. Freeze cut pieces on a cookie sheet for about an hour before frosting. Exposed cut edges may be crumb coated before frosting to help control crumbling. To do this, mix water, a teaspoon at a time, into a small amount of frosting, to make a thin frosting. Spread a smooth, thin layer onto cut surfaces; freeze.

Keep frostings covered with plastic wrap while working to prevent them from crusting and becoming dry.

Freezing Unfrosted and Frosted Cakes

Unfrosted cakes and cupcakes freeze better than frosted cakes. Allow the cakes to cool completely. Place cakes in rigid containers (such as cardboard bakery boxes) to prevent crushing, then cover with aluminum foil, plastic wrap or large freezer bags. Properly packaged, unfrosted cakes can be kept frozen 3 to 4 months. Cakes can also be frozen in family portions or single pieces that thaw out quickly.

Of the frosted cakes, those with creamy-type frostings freeze best. Fluffy-type and whipped cream frostings freeze well but tend to stick to the wrappings. To prevent frosting from sticking to the wrapping, freeze cake uncovered 1 hour, insert wooden picks around the top and side of cake, and wrap. Frozen frosted cakes keep for 2 to 3 months.

Decorating gel, hard candies and colored sugars do not freeze well. They tend to run during thawing.

Storing Unfrosted and Frosted Cakes

Cool unfrosted cakes completely before storing. If covered when warm, they become sticky. To store cakes that will be frosted later, cover them loosely so the surface stays dry. Otherwise, they become sticky and difficult to frost.

Store cakes with a creamy-type frosting under a cake safe (or large inverted bowl) or cover loosely with aluminum foil, plastic wrap or waxed paper.

Cakes with whipped cream toppings or cream fillings should be stored in the refrigerator.

Fluffy frostings are not as stable as creamy frostings because so much air is incorporated into them. It is best to frost a cake with fluffy frosting on the day it is to be served. However, if you must store the cake overnight, place it under a cake safe or inverted bowl and slip a wooden spoon handle or a knife blade under the rim so the cover is not airtight.

Cutting Frosted Cakes

Use a sharp, thin knife to cut shortening-type cakes and a long serrated knife for angels and chiffons. If the frosting sticks, dip the knife into hot water and wipe with a damp paper towel after cutting each slice. Cover exposed cut ends with plastic wrap to maintain moistness.

Backgrounds for Cut-Up Cakes

Cakes may be served on trays, large bread-boards or inverted jellyroll pans. If you do not have a tray large enough, use a piece of cardboard cut 2 to 4 inches larger than the assembled cake. Cover the background with aluminum or colored foil, colored plastic wrap or freezer paper. To vary the color or fit the occasion, use other paper, such as shelf paper, gift wrap, colored tissue paper or a home-drawn creation, and then cover with clear cellophane or plastic wrap. If you wish, messages or other designs can be added to the background around the cake with either a marking pencil or piped frosting.

Decorating Basics

1. It is important that the frosting to be used for decorating is the right consistency. Borders and drop flowers can have a medium consistency frosting, roses and other flowers need a firmer frosting so the petals will hold their shape and frosting to be used for writing, leaves and simple line designs can be slightly thinner.

2. Powdered sugar must be completely free of lumps when it is to be used for a decorating frosting. If there are even small lumps it will be necessary to sift it.

3. Most designs are made by holding the decorating bag at a 45° angle as shown in top right illustration. For drop flowers, stars, dots and rosettes, hold the bag at a 90° angle (perpendicular to the surface).

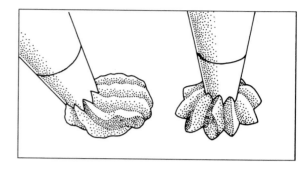

4. Before piping a design or a message on a cake, lightly outline the design with a wooden pick to use as a guide (see below). Short strips of sewing thread can be lightly placed on the frosted cake to mark the position of the message.

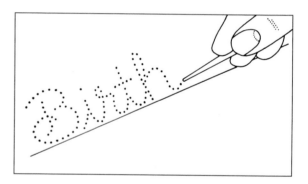

5. Use steady pressure to press out the frosting. The amount of pressure will determine the size and evenness of any design. To finish a design, stop the pressure and lift the point up and away.

CAKE YIELDS

Size and Type of Cake	Number of Servings
8-inch layer	10 to 14
9-inch layer	12 to 16
9-inch loaf	8 to 10
8- or 9-inch square	9
13 × 9-inch rectangular	12 to 15
10-inch tube	12 to 16
12-cup fluted tube	12 to 16

6. When adding food color, remember that frosting will darken slightly as it sets. For vivid or deeper food colors, use paste food color.

7. A turntable or lazy Susan is a helpful tool to make it easier and faster to frost and decorate cakes.

Decorating Bags

Decorating bags used for cake decorating include reusable plastic-coated decorating bags and disposable parchment paper or plastic bags. The plastic-coated decorating bag can be used with or without a coupler. The coupler saves time by enabling you to change decorating tips while still using the same bag of frosting. A coupler is not used for large decorating tips.

If you do not have a decorating bag, you can make a cone from a plastic bag or paper envelope. Place $1/2$ cup frosting in the corner of the bag and seal, or, place $1/3$ cup frosting in the corner of an envelope and fold the sides of the envelope toward the center. Snip a small piece off the corner to make a tip.

How to Fit Your New Decorating Bag with a Coupler

1. Unscrew the ring off the coupler base and drop the base, narrow end first, down into the end of the bag. Push the coupler base as far down into the bag as possible.

2. With a pencil, mark the location of the coupler's bottom thread on the outside of the bag. Push the coupler up and out of the bag.

3. Cut off the end of the decorating bag at the pencil mark. (Be careful not to cut too much; you can always trim a little more later if necessary.)

4. Replace the coupler base in the bag, pushing it down so the 2 bottom threads of the coupler show through the open end of the bag. Place decorating tip in ring and screw onto coupler base.

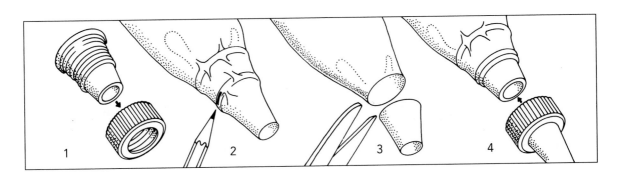

HOW TO USE YOUR DECORATING BAG

If not using a coupler or if the decorating tip is large, simply place the tip in the bag. If using a coupler, place the desired decorating tip on the coupler base and screw the coupler ring into place over the tip to hold it securely. With tip in place you're ready to fill the bag with frosting.

To fill the bag with frosting or whipped cream, fold down the open end of the bag to form a cuff approximately 2 inches wide. Hold the bag beneath the cuff and, using a spatula, fill the bag half full with frosting. (Don't fill the bag too full or frosting will back up out of the bag.)

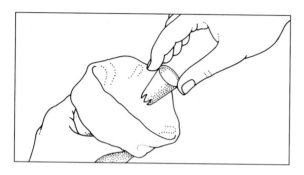

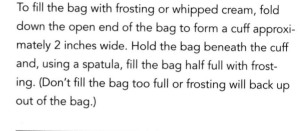

To close the bag, unfold the cuff and twist the top of the bag, forcing the frosting down into the tip. Continue to twist end of bag as you decorate.

To change decorating tips, unscrew the coupler ring, remove the tip, replace it with another tip and screw the ring on again.

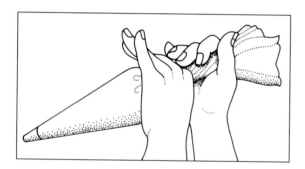

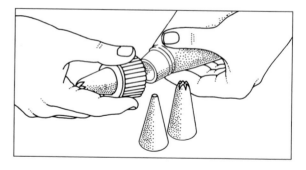

HOW TO MAKE ROSETTES

Using a star tip, press out whipped cream or frosting, using steady, even pressure, into a circle. Then, without stopping, spiral the whipped cream on top in a smaller circle, finally ending the swirl in a peak as you decrease the pressure.

HOW TO MAKE DROP FLOWERS

Using a drop flower tip, hold the decorating bag perpendicular (straight up) with the tip touching the surface. Squeeze the bag, keeping the tip in frosting until petals are formed. Stop pressure and pull away.

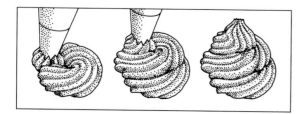

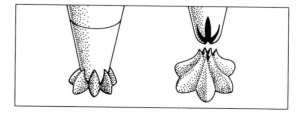

DECORATING TIPS AND THEIR USES

Drop Flower Tips   These tips make the easiest flowers for a beginning cake decorator. They are made directly on the frosted cake. The number of petals is determined by the number of openings in the end of the tip. Drop flower tips can be used to make either plain or swirled drop flowers. Popular drop flower tips include numbers 107, 129, 190, 217, 224, 225, 1C and 2D.

Leaf Tips   The **V**-shaped opening of this tip forms the pointed end of the leaf. Leaf tips make plain, ruffled or stand-up leaves. Leaf tips can also be used to make attractive borders. Popular leaf tips include 65, 67 and 352.

Petal Tips   These tips are used for making roses, wild roses, violets, sweet peas and carnations. They are also used for making ribbons, bows, swags and ruffles. Popular petal tips include numbers 101, 102, 103 and 104. For very large roses, number 127 can be used.

Star Tips   These tips are used for making shell, rope and zigzag borders, stars and rosettes and can also be used for making drop flowers. Popular star tips include numbers 13 through 22 and can range in size from small to very large. Large star tips include numbers 32, 43 and 8B.

Writing Tips   Writing tips are also called plain or round tips. In addition to writing messages, these tips can be used for making beads, dots, balls, stems, vines and flower centers. Popular writing tips include numbers 1 through 4 (small), 5 through 12 (medium) and 1A and 2A (large).

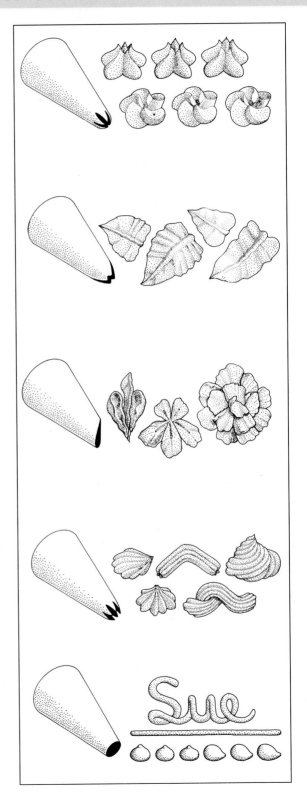

BORDERS

Shell Border   As the name implies, this is a series of shells connected in a continuous line. Using a star tip, hold decorating bag at a 45° angle to surface. Press out frosting using consistent heavy pressure to create a full base. Raise the tip as shell builds up. Decrease pressure, drawing frosting to a point. Begin the next shell directly over that point.

Reverse Shell Border   This border is similar to the plain Shell Border except that as the shell is built up, circle to the right and decrease pressure. The second shell is circled to the left. Continue, alternating shells from right to left.

Bead Border   This technique is the same as the Shell Border technique except uses a writing tip. Vary pressure to make different size balls.

Zigzag Border   Using a star or writing tip, hold the decorating bag at a 45° angle to surface. Press out frosting with a steady, even pressure, moving bag from side to side slightly to form a zigzag line.

Rope Border   Using a star or large writing tip, hold the decorating bag at a 45° angle to the surface. Touch the tip to the surface and squeeze the bag, moving the tip down, up and around to the right, forming a slight **S** curve. Stop pressure and pull the tip away. Place the tip under bottom curve of the first **S** and repeat the procedure. Continue joining **S** curves to form rope.

Swag Border   Using a star, petal or writing tip, hold the decorating bag at a 45° angle to the surface. As you press out frosting, move the tip down and up, down and up as if writing a continuous letter **S**. Use steady, even pressure as you repeat the procedure. When completed, discontinue pressure and pull the tip away.

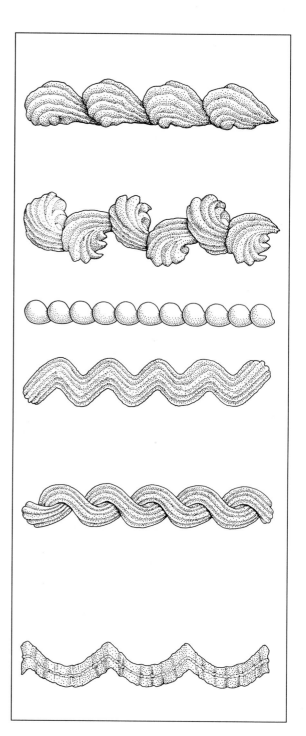

HOW TO MAKE A BASIC LEAF

Using a leaf tip, hold the decorating bag at an angle to the surface. Squeeze and hold tip in place to let the frosting fan out to form base of leaf. Decrease pressure as you slowly pull the tip away and lift slightly to draw the leaf to a point.

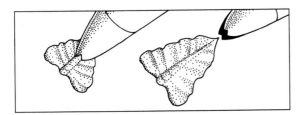

HOW TO USE A FLOWER NAIL

The flower nail is used to make flowers such as roses and marigolds. The frosting used to make flowers on a flower nail should be quite stiff.

To use a flower nail, attach a 2-inch square of waxed paper to the nail with a small dab of frosting. Hold the stem of the nail between the left thumb and forefinger and slowly rotate the nail to the left (counterclockwise). Hold the decorating bag in the right hand and press out frosting to form the petals. (Left-handed decorators should reverse these directions.)

Flowers can be made in advance and air dried or they can be placed directly on the cake.

HOW TO MAKE SIMPLE DESIGNS

Using a writing tip, hold the decorating bag at a 45° angle. With the tip raised slightly from the surface, squeeze the bag, applying pressure evenly, and direct the tip to outline the desired design. To end the design stop squeezing, touch tip to surface and pull away.

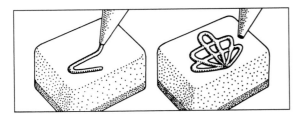

HOW TO MAKE MARIGOLDS

Touch the wide end of petal tip to center of flower nail, lifting narrow end slightly. Pipe a circle of narrow petals, each about 1/2 inch long, using a continuous back and forth motion. Turn the nail slowly as you pipe.

Pipe 2 or 3 more rows of petals, one on top of the other, making the petals in each row shorter than the last.

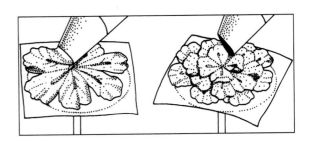

HOW TO MAKE ROSES

1. Using a petal tip, hold the bag with narrow end of the tip up. Turn the flower nail counterclockwise and press out frosting in a tiny circle to form center of rose.

2. To form the first petal, make a standing half circle to one side of center.

3. Add 2 more petals, forming a triangle.

4. Add more petals, overlapping, until rose is desired size. Remove the waxed paper with rose from the nail. Place on a level surface and let stand until set. Carefully lift the rose from waxed paper with a spatula and place on the cake. Attach with additional frosting if necessary.

NOTE: For very large roses, use tip #127.

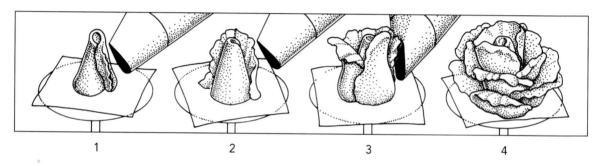

1   2   3   4

HOW TO MAKE WILD ROSES OR APPLE BLOSSOMS

1. Make a small flat circle of frosting in center of flower nail for base of flower (petals are to be connected securely to this).

2. Using a petal tip, hold the bag with wide end of tip touching center of nail and narrow end almost parallel to nail's surface. As you press out the first petal, turn the nail to the left and move the tip out to the edge of nail and back to center. Stop pressure at center to complete petal and move tip away.

3. Make 4 more petals the same way, always working to the right of the previous petal.

4. Change to a writing tip and hold the bag perpendicular (straight up) to the center of the flower. Press out 2 or 3 small dots at center.

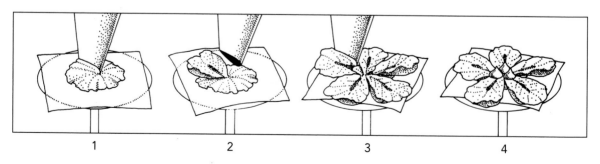

1   2   3   4

CHOCOLATE TIPS

Melting Chocolate

Chocolate can be easily melted on the stovetop or in the microwave. Melting must be done carefully, however, as any amount of steam or water will cause the chocolate to harden or "tighten" which is known as "seizing." Chocolate chips can be melted as they are; bars or squares of chocolate should be broken or chopped before melting.

- Heat chocolate in a heavy saucepan over low heat, stirring occasionally, until almost melted. Remove from heat and stir until completely melted.

- Place chocolate in a small, heatproof bowl in hot water or top of a double boiler over hot (not boiling) water, stirring occasionally, until melted.

- Microwave $^1/_2$ to 1 cup chocolate chips uncovered on medium (50%) 3 to $4^1/_2$ minutes, 1 or 2 squares 3 or 4 minutes, stirring after $2^1/_2$ minutes. Stir until smooth.

Chocolate Pointers

"Seizing" is the term used when a very small amount of moisture causes chocolate to become thick, lumpy and grainy during melting. Be sure all utensils are completely dry and that no moisture gets into the chocolate while it melts.

Chocolate can be returned to a creamy consistency by stirring in about 1 teaspoon shortening for each ounce of chocolate being melted.

"Bloom" is the term for the dusty looking film that develops on chocolate stored at room temperatures that vary from hot to cold, allowing the cocoa butter to melt and rise to the surface of the chocolate. It does not affect the flavor or quality of the chocolate.

Chocolate Storage

To maintain good quality, chocolate must be stored properly. It is important to store it in a cool, dry place between 60° and 78°. If the temperature is higher than 78° or the humidity is above 50 percent, chocolate should be kept wrapped in moistureproof wrap. Chocolate can be stored in the refrigerator if tightly wrapped to keep out moisture and odors. Cold chocolate becomes hard and brittle, so remove it from the refrigerator and let stand at room temperature before using.

Cocoa is less sensitive to temperature and humidity than chocolate. It is best to store cocoa in a tightly covered container in a cool, dry place.

CHOCOLATE EQUIVALENTS

1 package (6 ounces) semisweet chocolate chips	1 cup semisweet chocolate chips
1 package (8 ounces) unsweetened chocolate	8 squares (1 ounce chocolate each) unsweetened chocolate
1 envelope (1 ounce) premelted chocolate	1 square (1 ounce) unsweetened chocolate
1 square (1 ounce) unsweetened chocolate, melted	3 tablespoons unsweetened cocoa plus 1 tablespoon vegetable oil or shortening
3 squares (1 ounce each) semisweet chocolate	$^1/_2$ cup semisweet chocolate chips

Chocolate Curls

Place a bar or block of chocolate on waxed paper. Make curls by pressing firmly against the chocolate and pulling a vegetable peeler toward you in long, thin strokes. Small curls can be made by using the side of the chocolate bar. Transfer each curl carefully with a wooden pick to a waxed paper-lined cookie sheet or directly onto frosted cake.

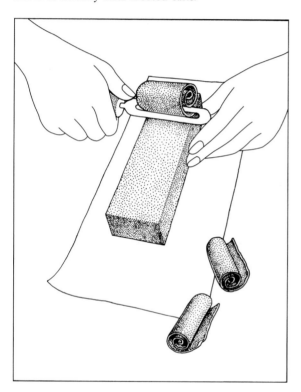

The curls will be easier to make if the chocolate is slightly warm. Let the chocolate stand in a warm place for about 15 minutes before slicing. Semisweet chocolate can be used, but curls will be smaller. Thicker bars of chocolate will make larger curls.

Chocolate Cut-Outs

Melt 1 bar (4 ounces) sweet cooking chocolate or 4 squares (1 ounce each) semisweet chocolate. Spread over outside bottom of square pan, 8 × 8 × 2 inches. Refrigerate until firm; bring to room temperature. Use cookie cutters in desired shapes and sizes to make cut-outs. Refrigerate until ready to place on dessert. Make your cut-outs extra special by dipping half of each cut-out in melted white chocolate and refrigerating until set.

Chocolate Ribbons

Melt 4 ounces white chocolate (white baking bar) or semisweet chocolate. Spread with a metal spatula in a thin layer on a large cookie sheet. Refrigerate about 10 minutes or *just* until chocolate is firm. (Do not refrigerate until hard or chocolate will break. If chocolate gets too hard, let stand at room temperature.)

Scrape strips of chocolate with a knife or metal pastry scraper. Hold the knife flat to the sheet and pull slowly toward you, curling ribbons as you go. (See photo of Apricot-Almond Wedding Cake on page 87.)

Chocolate Twigs

Melt 2 ounces white chocolate (white baking bar) or 2 ounces semisweet chocolate and 1 teaspoon shortening. Pour into decorating bag with small writing tip. Squeeze melted chocolate onto waxed paper into twig shapes; sprinkle with white decorator's sugar, if desired. Let dry. Peel twigs from waxed paper; arrange on cake.

Shaved Chocolate

All types of chocolate can be used to make shaved chocolate. Slide a vegetable peeler across the surface of a bar or block of chocolate, using short, quick strokes. Or, use a vegetable shredder with large holes. Sprinkle on frosted cake.

ANGEL FOOD CAKE

1^1/$_2$ cups powdered sugar
1 cup cake flour
1^1/$_2$ cups egg whites (about 12)
1^1/$_2$ teaspoons cream of tartar
1 cup granulated sugar
1^1/$_2$ teaspoons vanilla
^{1}/$_2$ teaspoon almond extract
^{1}/$_4$ teaspoon salt

MOVE oven rack to lowest position. Heat oven to 375°. Mix powdered sugar and flour. Beat egg whites and cream of tartar in large bowl on medium speed until foamy. Beat in granulated sugar on high speed, 2 tablespoons at a time, adding vanilla, almond extract and salt with the last addition of sugar. Continue beating until stiff and glossy. Do not underbeat.

SPRINKLE sugar-flour mixture, ^{1}/$_4$ cup at a time, over meringue, folding in just until sugar-flour mixture disappears. Push batter into ungreased tube pan, 10 × 4 inches. Cut gently through batter with metal spatula.

BAKE 30 to 35 minutes or until cracks in cake feel dry and top springs back when touched lightly. Immediately turn pan upside down onto glass bottle or metal funnel. Let hang about 2 hours or until cake is completely cool. Remove from pan. Spread top of cake with White Chocolate Glaze (page 153) if desired.

Chocolate Angel Food Cake Substitute ^{1}/$_4$ cup cocoa for ^{1}/$_4$ cup of the flour. Omit almond extract.

Spicy Angel Food Cake Add 1 teaspoon pumpkin pie spice with flour. Omit almond extract.

APPLESAUCE CAKE

2^1/$_2$ cups all-purpose flour or cake flour
1^1/$_4$ cups sugar
1^1/$_2$ teaspoons baking soda
1^1/$_2$ teaspoons salt
^{3}/$_4$ teaspoon ground cinnamon
^{1}/$_2$ teaspoon ground cloves
^{1}/$_2$ teaspoon ground allspice
^{1}/$_4$ teaspoon baking powder
1^1/$_2$ cups applesauce
^{1}/$_2$ cup water
^{1}/$_2$ cup shortening
2 eggs
1 cup raisins
^{1}/$_2$ cup chopped walnuts

HEAT oven to 350°. Grease and flour desired pan(s). Beat all ingredients in large bowl on low speed 30 seconds, scraping bowl constantly. Beat on high speed 3 minutes, scraping bowl occasionally. Pour batter into pan(s).

BAKE as directed below or until toothpick inserted in center comes out clean. Cool 10 minutes; remove from pan(s). Cool completely.

13 × 9 × 2 inch rectangle	55 to 60 minutes
two 8 × 1^1/$_2$-inch rounds	50 to 55 minutes
two 9 × 1^1/$_2$-inch rounds	50 to 55 minutes
9 × 1^1/$_2$-inch round	50 to 55 minutes
6 × 3-inch ovenproof bowl	70 to 80 minutes

Whole Wheat Applesauce Cake
Substitute 1^1/$_4$ cups whole wheat flour for 1^1/$_4$ cups of the all-purpose flour. Do not use cake flour.

B U T T E R M I L K   S P I C E   C A K E

$2^{1}/2$ cups all-purpose flour or cake flour
1 cup granulated sugar
$^{3}/4$ cup packed brown sugar
$^{1}/2$ cup shortening
$1^{1}/3$ cups buttermilk
1 teaspoon baking powder
1 teaspoon baking soda
1 teaspoon salt
$^{3}/4$ teaspoon ground cinnamon
$^{3}/4$ teaspoon ground allspice
$^{1}/2$ teaspoon ground cloves
$^{1}/2$ teaspoon ground nutmeg
3 eggs

HEAT oven to 350°. Grease and flour desired pan(s). Beat all ingredients in large bowl on medium speed 30 seconds, scraping bowl constantly. Beat on high speed 3 minutes, scraping bowl occasionally. Pour batter into pan(s).

BAKE as directed below or until toothpick inserted in center comes out clean. Cool 10 minutes; remove from pan(s). Cool completely.

13 × 9 × 2-inch rectangle	40 to 45 minutes
$15^{1}/2$ × $10^{1}/2$ × 1-inch jelly roll	30 to 35 minutes
two 8 × $1^{1}/2$-inch rounds	40 to 45 minutes
two 9 × $1^{1}/2$-inch rounds	35 to 40 minutes

C A R R O T   C A K E

$1^{1}/2$ cups sugar
1 cup vegetable oil
3 eggs
2 cups all-purpose flour
$1^{1}/2$ teaspoons ground cinnamon
1 teaspoon baking soda
1 teaspoon vanilla
$^{1}/2$ teaspoon salt
$^{1}/4$ teaspoon ground nutmeg
3 cups shredded carrots (about 5 medium)
1 cup coarsely chopped nuts

HEAT oven to 350°. Grease and flour desired pan(s). Mix sugar, oil and eggs in large bowl until blended; beat 1 minute. Stir in remaining ingredients except carrots and nuts; beat 1 minute. Stir in carrots and nuts. Pour batter into pan(s).

BAKE as directed below or until toothpick inserted in center comes out clean. Cool 10 minutes; remove from pan(s). Cool completely.

13 × 9 × 2-inch rectangle	35 to 40 minutes
two 8 × $1^{1}/2$-inch rounds	40 to 45 minutes
two 9 × $1^{1}/2$-inch rounds	35 to 40 minutes

Apple Cake: Substitute 3 cups chopped tart apples (about 3 medium) for the carrots.

DARK COCOA CAKE

2^1/4 cups all-purpose flour
1^2/3 cups sugar
^{2}/3 cup cocoa
^{3}/4 cup shortening
1^1/4 cups water
1^1/4 teaspoons baking soda
1 teaspoon salt
^{1}/4 teaspoon baking powder
1 teaspoon vanilla
2 eggs

HEAT oven to 350°. Grease and flour desired pan(s). Beat all ingredients in large bowl on low speed 30 seconds, scraping bowl constantly. Beat on high speed 3 minutes, scraping bowl occasionally. Pour batter into pan(s).

BAKE as directed below or until toothpick inserted in center comes out clean. Cool 10 minutes; remove from pan(s). Cool completely.

13 × 9 × 2-inch rectangle	40 to 45 minutes
two 8 × 1^1/2-inch rounds	35 to 40 minutes
two 9 × 1^1/2-inch rounds	30 to 35 minutes
two 8 × 8 × 2-inch squares	35 to 40 minutes
24 medium 2^1/2 × 1^1/4-inch muffin cups	20 to 25 minutes

DOUBLE CHOCOLATE CAKE

2^1/4 cups all-purpose flour
1^3/4 cups sugar
^{1}/2 cup shortening
1^1/2 cups buttermilk
1^1/2 teaspoons baking soda
1 teaspoon salt
1 teaspoon vanilla
2 ounces unsweetened chocolate, melted and cooled
2 eggs
1 cup miniature chocolate chips

HEAT oven to 350°. Grease and flour desired pan(s). Beat all ingredients except chocolate in large bowl on medium speed 30 seconds, scraping bowl constantly. Beat on high speed 2 minutes, scraping bowl occasionally. Fold in chocolate chips. Pour batter into pan(s).

BAKE as directed below or until toothpick inserted in center comes out clean. Cool 10 minutes; remove from pan(s). Cool completely.

13 × 9 × 2-inch rectangle	40 to 45 minutes
two 9 × 5 × 3-inch loaves	35 to 40 minutes
two 8 × 1^1/2-inch rounds	40 to 45 minutes
two 9 × 1^1/2-inch rounds	35 to 40 minutes
two 9 × 9 × 2-inch squares	35 to 40 minutes
24 medium 2^1/2 × 1^1/4-inch muffin cups	20 to 25 minutes

Chocolate-Cherry Cake: Fold in ^{1}/2 cup chopped maraschino cherries, well drained, with the chocolate chips.

BASIC CAKES

POUND CAKE

2 cups all-purpose flour

1 cup sugar

3 teaspoons baking powder

$^1/_2$ teaspoon salt

$^1/_4$ cup ($^1/_2$ stick) margarine or butter, softened

$^1/_4$ cup shortening

$^3/_4$ cup milk

1 teaspoon vanilla

2 eggs

HEAT oven to 300°. Grease and flour desired pan(s). Beat all ingredients in large bowl on medium speed 30 seconds, scraping bowl constantly. Beat on high speed 2 minutes, scraping bowl occasionally. Pour batter into pan(s).

BAKE as directed below or until toothpick inserted in center comes out clean. Cool 10 minutes; remove from pan(s). Cool completely.

two 9 × 5 × 3-inch squares	40 to 45 minutes
1$^1/_2$-quart round casserole	65 to 75 minutes

PUMPKIN-GINGERBREAD CAKE

$3^1/_2$ cups all-purpose flour

2 cups sugar

1 cup (2 sticks) margarine or butter, softened

$^1/_2$ cup light molasses

$^1/_3$ cup water

2 teaspoons baking soda

1 teaspoon salt

1 teaspoon ground cinnamon

1 teaspoon ground ginger

$^1/_2$ teaspoon baking powder

$^1/_4$ teaspoon ground nutmeg

$^1/_4$ teaspoon ground cloves

1 can (1 lb) pumpkin

4 eggs

HEAT oven to 350°. Grease and flour desired pan(s). Beat all ingredients in large bowl on low speed 30 seconds, scraping bowl constantly. Beat on medium speed 3 minutes, scraping bowl occasionally. Pour batter into pan(s).

BAKE as directed below or until toothpick inserted in center comes out clean. Cool 10 minutes; remove from pan(s). Cool completely.

13 × 9 × 2-inch rectangle	50 to 55 minutes
two 1$^1/_2$-quart round casseroles	60 to 75 minutes

WHITE CAKE

2^1/$_4$ cups all-purpose flour
1^2/$_3$ cups sugar
^{2}/$_3$ cup shortening
1^1/$_4$ cups milk
3^1/$_2$ teaspoons baking powder
1 teaspoon salt
1 teaspoon vanilla
5 egg whites

HEAT oven to 350°. Grease and flour desired pan(s). (Line small muffin cups with paper baking cups.) Beat all ingredients except egg whites in large bowl on low speed 30 seconds, scraping bowl constantly. Beat on high speed 2 minutes, scraping bowl occasionally. Beat in egg whites on high speed 2 minutes, scraping bowl occasionally. Pour batter into pan(s).

BAKE as directed below or until toothpick inserted in center comes out clean or until cake springs back when touched lightly in center. Cool 10 minutes; remove from pan(s). Cool completely.

13 × 9 × 2-inch rectangle	40 to 45 minutes
15^1/$_2$ × 10^1/$_2$ × 1-inch jelly roll	25 to 30 minutes
two 8 × 1^1/$_2$-inch rounds	35 to 40 minutes
two 9 × 1^1/$_2$-inch rounds	30 to 35 minutes
12-cup ovenproof ring mold	35 to 40 minutes
24 medium 2^1/$_2$ × 1^1/$_4$-inch muffin cups	20 to 25 minutes
12 small 1^3/$_4$ × 1-inch muffin cups	10 to 15 minutes
8 × 1^1/$_2$-inch round and	30 to 35 minutes
8 × 8 × 2-inch square	30 to 35 minutes

BAKING PAN TIPS

If the recipe makes 36 cupcakes and you have only one 12-cup muffin pan or if you want to make a 3-layer cake and you have only 2 pans, cover and refrigerate the remaining batter while the first cupcakes or layers are baking.

Almond Cake: Substitute 1 teaspoon almond extract for the vanilla.

Cherry-Nut Cake: Fold ^{1}/$_2$ cup chopped nuts and ^{1}/$_3$ cup chopped maraschino cherries, well drained, into batter.

Hazelnut Cake: Add 1 cup ground hazelnuts with ingredients.

Marble Cake: Pour half of batter into another bowl. Mix 2 ounces unsweetened chocolate, melted and cooled, 1 tablespoon sugar, 2 tablespoons warm water and ^{1}/$_4$ teaspoon baking soda. Stir into one batter. Spoon light and dark batters alternately into pan(s). Cut through batter several times for marbled effect.

Pastel Marble Cake Divide batter into 3 equal parts. Tint one part with 2 or 3 drops red food color and one part with 2 or 3 drops green food color; leave other part plain. Spoon batters alternately into pan(s).

YELLOW CAKE

2 1/4 cups all-purpose flour
1 1/2 cups sugar
3 1/2 teaspoons baking powder
1 teaspoon salt
1 1/4 cups milk
1/4 cup (1/2 stick) margarine or butter, softened
1/4 cup shortening
1 teaspoon vanilla
3 eggs

HEAT oven to 350°. Grease and flour desired pan(s). Beat all ingredients in large bowl on low speed 30 seconds, scraping bowl constantly. Beat on high speed 3 minutes, scraping bowl occasionally. Pour batter into pan(s).

BAKE as directed below or until toothpick inserted in center comes out clean or until cake springs back when touched lightly in center. Cool 10 minutes; remove from pan(s). Cool completely.

13 × 9 × 2-inch rectangle	40 to 45 minutes
two 8 × 1 1/2-inch rounds	30 to 35 minutes
two 9 × 1 1/2-inch rounds	30 to 35 minutes
two 9 × 1 1/2-inch hearts	25 to 30 minutes
2-quart round casserole	65 to 75 minutes
12 medium 2 1/2 × 1 1/4-inch muffin cups and	20 to 25 minutes
9 × 9 × 2-inch square	30 to 35 minutes

Orange-Coconut Cake: Omit vanilla. Add 1 tablespoon grated orange peel and 1 cup flaked coconut with ingredients.

Lemon–Poppy Seed Cake: Omit vanilla. Add 1 tablespoon grated lemon peel and 2 tablespoons poppy seed with ingredients.

BUTTERCREAM FROSTING

8 cups powdered sugar
1 cup (2 sticks) margarine or butter, softened
1 cup shortening
1/3 cup milk
2 teaspoons vanilla or almond extract

BEAT powdered sugar, margarine and shortening in large bowl on low speed until blended. Beat in milk and vanilla on medium speed until smooth. If necessary, stir in milk, a few drops at a time, until of spreading consistency. *About 6 cups.*

CHOCOLATE DECORATOR FROSTING

1 square (1 ounce) unsweetened chocolate, chopped
1 teaspoon margarine or butter
1 cup powdered sugar
1 to 2 tablespoons boiling water

HEAT chocolate and margarine in 1-quart saucepan over low heat until melted; remove from heat. Blend in powdered sugar and 1 tablespoon water. Beat until smooth. Beat in additional water, 1 teaspoon at a time, until of spreading consistency. *About 1 cup.*

CREAMY CHOCOLATE FROSTING

1/2 cup (1 stick) margarine or butter, softened
3 ounces unsweetened chocolate, melted and cooled
3 cups powdered sugar
2 teaspoons vanilla
About 3 tablespoons milk

MIX margarine and chocolate in large bowl. Stir in powdered sugar. Beat in vanilla and milk until smooth and of spreading consistency. *About 2 1/4 cups.*

Creamy Cocoa Frosting: Substitute 1/2 cup cocoa for the chocolate.

CREAMY VANILLA FROSTING

5 1/2 cups powdered sugar
2/3 cup margarine or butter, softened
2 teaspoons vanilla
About 3 tablespoons milk

MIX powdered sugar and margarine in large bowl. Stir in vanilla and milk. Beat until smooth and of spreading consistency. *About 3 cups.*

Creamy Almond Frosting: Substitute 1 1/2 teaspoons almond extract for the vanilla.

Creamy Citrus Frosting: Omit vanilla. Substitute lemon or orange juice for the milk. Stir in 1/2 teaspoon grated lemon peel or 2 teaspoons grated orange peel.

Peanut Butter Frosting: Substitute peanut butter for the margarine. Increase milk to 1/4 to 1/3 cup.

CREAMY WHITE FROSTING

REGULAR VANILLA extract will work in this recipe, but clear vanilla will make for a whiter frosting. It is available at large supermarkets or specialty baking shops.

6 cups powdered sugar
3/4 cup shortening
Milk
3/4 teaspoon clear vanilla or almond extract

MIX powdered sugar and shortening in large bowl. Beat in milk and vanilla until smooth. If necessary, stir in milk, a few drops at a time, until of spreading consistency. *About 4 cups.*

CREAM CHEESE FROSTING

1 package (8 ounces) cream cheese, softened
1 tablespoon milk
1 teaspoon vanilla
4 cups powdered sugar

BEAT cream cheese, milk and vanilla in large bowl on low speed until smooth. Gradually beat in powdered sugar, 1 cup at a time, until smooth and of spreading consistency. Refrigerate any remaining frosted cake. *About 2 1/2 cups.*

EASY PENUCHE FROSTING

¹/₂ cup (1 stick) margarine or butter
1 cup packed brown sugar
¹/₄ cup milk
2 cups powdered sugar

HEAT margarine in 1¹/₂-quart saucepan over low heat until melted. Stir in brown sugar. Heat to boiling, stirring constantly. Boil and stir over low heat 2 minutes. Stir in milk. Heat to boiling; remove from heat. Cool to lukewarm. Gradually stir in powdered sugar. Place saucepan in bowl of ice and water; beat until of spreading consistency. If frosting becomes too stiff, heat slightly, stirring constantly. *About 2 cups.*

WHITE DECORATOR FROSTING

6¹/₄ cups powdered sugar
³/₄ cup shortening
¹/₂ cup milk
³/₄ teaspoon clear vanilla or almond extract

MIX powdered sugar and shortening. Beat in milk and vanilla until smooth. If necessary, stir in additional milk, a few drops at a time, until of spreading consistency. *About 4 cups.*

WHITE MOUNTAIN FROSTING

¹/₂ cup sugar
¹/₄ cup light corn syrup
2 tablespoons water
2 egg whites
1 teaspoon vanilla

MIX sugar, corn syrup and water in 1-quart saucepan. cover and heat to rolling boil over medium heat. Uncover and boil rapidly to 242° on candy thermometer (or until small amount of mixture dropped into very cold water forms a firm ball that holds its shape until pressed).

AS mixture boils, beat egg whites in medium bowl just until stiff peaks form. Pour hot syrup very slowly in thin stream into egg whites, beating constantly on medium speed. Add vanilla; beat on high speed until stiff peaks form. *About 3 cups.*

Note: To get an accurate temperature reading on the thermometer, it may be necessary to tilt the saucepan slightly. It takes 4 to 8 minutes for the syrup to reach 242°. Preparing this type of frosting on a humid day may require a longer beating time.

Fluffy Brown Sugar Frosting: Substitute packed brown sugar for the granulated sugar and decrease vanilla to ¹/₂ teaspoon.

Fluffy Cocoa Frosting: Sift ¹/₄ cup cocoa over frosting and fold in until blended.

Fluffy Citrus Frosting: Substitute 1 teaspoon finely shredded orange or lemon peel for the vanilla.

BASIC GLAZES

CHOCOLATE GLAZE

1 package (6 ounces) semisweet chocolate chips
¹/₄ cup (¹/₂ stick) margarine or butter
2 tablespoons light corn syrup

HEAT all ingredients over low heat, stirring constantly, until chocolate chips are melted and mixture is smooth and of drizzling consistency. Cool slightly. *About 1 cup.*

WHITE CHOCOLATE GLAZE

¹/₂ cup vanilla milk chips
2 tablespoons light corn syrup
1¹/₂ teaspoons water

HEAT all ingredients over low heat, stirring constantly, until vanilla chips are melted and mixture is smooth and of drizzling consistency. Cool slightly. *About ¹/₂ cup.*

PETITS FOURS GLAZE

8 cups powdered sugar
¹/₂ cup water
¹/₂ cup light corn syrup
2 teaspoons almond extract

MIX all ingredients in top of double boiler until smooth. Heat just until lukewarm; remove from heat. Let glaze remain over hot water to prevent thickening. If necessary, add hot water, a few drops at a time, for desired consistency. *About 4 cups.*

INDEX

Numbers in *italics* refer to photos and illustrations.

A

Almond Cake, 149
Angel Food Cake, 145
    cooling and removing from
        pan, *134*, 134
    fall, *79*, 79
    splitting into layers, *134*, 134
Anniversary Cake, 90, *91*
Apple blossoms, how to make,
    141, 141
Applesauce Cake, 145
Apricot-Almond Wedding Cake,
    86–88, *87*
Athletic Shoe Cake, 11, *12*
Automobile Cake, *12*, 13

B

Baby Bib Shower Cake, *94*, 94
Backgrounds for cut-up cakes,
    136
Ballet Slippers Cake, 14–15, *15*
Baseball Cake, 40, *41*
Basic cakes
    almond, 149
    angel food, 145
    applesauce, 145
    buttermilk spice, 146
    carrot, 146
    cherry-nut, 149
    dark cocoa, 147
    double chocolate, 147
    hazelnut, 149
    marble, 149

    pastel marble, 149
    pound, 148
    pumpkin-gingerbread, 148
    white, 149
    yellow, 150
Basic leaf, how to make, *141*, 141
Batter, cake, beating, 131
Bear cakes
    -on-the-Bus Cake, *16*, 17
    panda, 38, *39*
    teddy, 46, *47*
Bicycle Cake, 18–19, *19*
Big Burger Cake, *20*, 21
Birthday cakes, 98, *99*
"Birthday-saurus" Bash Cake,
    96–97, *97*
Black Cat Cake, *72*, 73
"Bloom", definition of, 143
Boat, sail-, cake, *42*, 43
Bootie Shower Cakes, *94*, 95
Borders, basics of, 140
Browned Butter Glaze, 124
Bûche de Noël cakes, mini, *54*, 55
Bunny Cake, *8*, 10
    Easter, 64–65, *65*
Burger, big, cake, *20*, 21
Bus, bears-on-the, cake, *16*, 17
Butter, about, 131
Buttercream frosting, 150
Butterflies, candy designs, 26
Buttermilk
    maple-, cake, 118
    spice cake, 146

C

Cake basics
    angel food
        cooling and removing from
            pan, *134*, 134
        splitting into layers, *134*, 134
    baking tips, 131
    batter, beating, 131
    chiffon
        cooling and removing from
            pan, *134*, 134
        splitting into layers, *134*,
            134
    cut-up, cutting and frosting,
        135
    freezing, 135
    frosted, cutting, 135
    layers
        frosting, *133*, 133
        removing from pans, *132*,
            132
        splitting, *132*, 132
    storing, 135
    yields, 137
Cake Full of Hearts, *62*, 63
Candy butterflies, 26
Caramel Cake, 114
Caramel frosting, 114
Caramel-Pecan Torte, 114, *115*
Carrot Cake, 146
Cat
    black, cake, *72*, 73
    gumdrop design, 75
    kitty, cake, *23*, 24

INDEX

Celebration cakes
    anniversary, 90, *91*
    anniversary and shower,
        90–91, *91*
    apricot-almond wedding,
        86–88, *87*
    baby bib shower, *94*, 94
    birthday, 98, *99*
    "birthday-saurus" bash, 96–97,
        97
    bootie shower, *94*, 95
    classic white wedding, *82*,
        84–85
    computer, *104*, 105
    double-ring shower, 90–91, *91*
    Father's Day T-shirt, *102*,
        102–3
    flower silhouette birthday, 98,
        99
    gone fishin', 106, *107*
    happy birthday, 98, *99*
    housewarming, 106, *107*
    Mother's Day straw hat,
        100–101, *101*
    petits fours, *89*, 89
    Star of David, 108, *109*
    umbrella, 92, *93*
Cheese and Mouse Cake, 22, *23*
Cherry-Nut Cake, 149
Chiffon cake
    cooling and removing from
        pan, *134*, 134
    peppermint, 128
    splitting into layers, *134*, 134
Chocolate
    curls, *144*, 144
    cut-outs, 144
    decorator frosting, 150
    -dipped nuts or fruits, 114

equivalents, 143
feather design, 21
flower design, 30
frosting
    creamy, 151
    mint, 128
glaze, 153
leaves, 78
melting, 143
ribbons, 144
shaved, 144
tips, 143–44
twigs, 144
web design, 75
Chocolate cakes
    Chocolate Cookie Cake, *115*,
        116
    decadent, *116*, 117
    double, 147
    Chocolate Heart Cake, 61, *62*
    Chocolate Mint Loaves, *127*,
        128
Christmas designs, 55
Christmas Tree Cake, 53, *54*
Coating sides of cake, 118
Cocoa cake, dark, 147
Cocoa frostings, 151, 152
Coconut, orange-, cake, 150
Computer Cake, *104*, 105
Cookie-Sour Cream Cake, 116
Cooling and removing cakes
    from pan, *134*, 134
Cornucopia garnishes, 78
Coupler, fitting new decorating
    bag with a, 137
Cream cheese frosting, 151
Cross, Easter, cake, 66–67, *67*
Curls, chocolate, *144*, 144

Custard cream filling, 112
Custard-filled Nutmeg Cake, *111*,
    112
Cut-out and shaped cakes
    athletic shoe, 11, *12*
    automobile, *12*, 13
    backgrounds for, 136
    ballet slippers, 14–15, *15*
    baseball, 40, *41*
    bears-on-the-bus, *16*, 17
    bicycle, 18–19, *19*
    big burger, *20*, 21
    bunny, *8*, 10
    cheese and mouse, 22, *23*
    cutting and frosting, 135
    dinosaur, 26–27, *27*
    electric guitar, 28–29, *29*
    fish, 30–31, *31*
    gum ball machine, 32, *33*
    horse's head, *34*, 35
    in-line skate, 36–37, *37*
    kitty cat, *23*, 24
    monkey, *34*, 35, 36
    panda, 38, *39*
    play ball, 40, *41*
    sailboat, *42*, 43
    snowman, 25
    spaceship, 44, *45*
    teddy bear, 46, *47*
    train, 48–49, *49*
Cut-outs, chocolate, 144
Cutting and frosting cut-up
    cakes, 135

D

Dark Cocoa Cake, 147
Decadent Chocolate Cake, *116*,
    117

INDEX

Decorating bags, *137*, 137, *138*, 138

    fitting with a coupler, 137

    how to use, *138*, 138

Decorating basics, *136*, 136

Decorating tips and their uses, 139

Design. *See also* Flower designs; Gumdrop designs

    cakes in bloom, 88

    Christmas, 55

    cookie cutter, 63

    feather, 15

    filled-in, 63

    ghost, marshmallow, 75

    holiday, 55

    outlined, 63

    patchwork, 41

    plaid, 15

    President's Day, 70

    simple, how to make, *141*, 141

    stencil, 97

    tic-tac-toe, 15

    web, chocolate, 75

Dinosaur Cake, 26–27, *27*

    "Birthday-saurus" Bash Cake, 96–97, *97*

Double Chocolate Cake, 147

Double-Ring Shower Cake, 90–91, *91*

Dowels, use of, 134

Dreidel, Hanukkah, cake, 80–81, *81*

Drop flower

    making, *138*, 138

    tips, *139*, 139

Dry ingredients, measuring, 130

E

Easter Bunny Cake, 64–65, *65*

Easter Cross Cake, 66–67, *67*

Easy penuche frosting, 152

Eggs, about, 131

Electric Guitar Cake, 28–29, *29*

F

Fall Angel Food Cake, *79*, 79

Father's Day T-Shirt Cake, *102*, 102–3

Filled-in designs, 63

Filling, custard cream, 112

Firecracker Cakes, *70*, 70

Fish Cake, 30–31, *31*

Flower designs. *See also* Drop Flower; Rose designs

    drop, making, *138*, 138

    fresh flower decorations, 88

    marshmallow, 90

    whipped cream rosettes, 88

Flower nail, how to use, *141*, 141

Flower Silhouette Birthday Cake, 98, *99*

Freezing unfrosted and frosted cakes, 135

French Silk Hazelnut Cake, *110*, 113

Frosted cakes, tips for, 135

Frosting

    almond, creamy, 151

    basic, 150, 151–152

    brown sugar, 152

    buttercream, 150

    caramel, 114

    chocolate, creamy, 151

    chocolate decorator, 150

    chocolate-mint, 128

    citrus, creamy, 151

    citrus, fluffy, 152

    cocoa, creamy, 151

    cocoa, fluffy, 152

    cream cheese, 151

    easy penuche, 152

    French silk, 113

    maple-butter, 118

    mocha cream, 122

    peanut butter, 151

    vanilla, creamy, 151

    whipped cream cheese, 119

    white, creamy, 151

    white decorator, 152

    white mountain, 152

Frosting tips

    cut-up cakes, 135

    layer cakes, *133*, 133

Fruit

    chocolate-dipped, 114

    fresh fruit decorations, 121

Fruitcake

    glazed whole wheat, 124, *125*

    mincemeat, 124

    ring, 124, *125*

G

Gingerbread cakes

    cottage, 58–59, *59*

    pumpkin-, 148

Glazed Whole Wheat Fruitcake, 124, *125*

Glazes

    browned butter, 124

    chocolate, 153

    Petits Fours, 153

    white chocolate, 153

INDEX

Golden Pound Cake, 127
Gone Fishin' Cake, 106, *107*
Guitar, electric, cake, 28–29, *29*
Gum Ball Machine Cake, 32, *33*
Gumdrop designs
    cat, 75
    hatchets, 70
    holly, 55
    rose, 88
    spider, 75

H
Halloween Haunters, 75
Hanukkah Dreidel Cake, 80–81, *81*
Happy Birthday Cake, 98, *99*
Hazelnut Cake, 149
    French silk, *111*, 113
Heart cake
    chocolate, 61, *62*
    Cake Full of Hearts, *62*, 63
Holiday cakes
    black cat, 72, 73
    Cake Full of Hearts, *62*, 63
    chocolate heart, 61, *62*
    Christmas tree, 53, *54*
    Easter bunny, 64–65, *65*
    Easter cross, 66–67, *67*
    fall angel food, *79*, 79
    firecracker, *70*, 70
    Gingerbread Cake Cottage, 58–59, *59*
    Hanukkah dreidel, 80–81, *81*
    holiday pinecone, *50*, 52
    holiday quilt, *56*, 56
    jack-o'-lantern, *71*, 71
    let's celebrate, 60, *60*

mini bûche de Noël cakes, *54*, 55
peppermint whipped cream, *56*, 57
pot-o'-gold, 68–69, *69*
spiderweb, *74*, 74
Thanksgiving, 77, 78
turkey gobbler, 76, *77*
Holiday Pinecone Cake, *50*, 52
Holiday Quilt Cake, *56*, 56
Horse's Head Cake, *34*, 35
Housewarming Cake, 106, *107*

I
In-Line Skate Cake, 36–37, *37*
Ingredients, measuring, 130

J
Jack-o'-Lantern Cake, *71*, 71

K
Kitty Cat Cake, *23*, 24

L
Layer cake
    frosting, *133*, 133
    removing from pans, *132*, 132
    yields, 85
Leaf tips, *139*, 139
Leaves, chocolate, 78
Lemon Meringue Cake, 120, *121*
Lemon-Poppy Seed Cake, 150
Let's Celebrate Cake, *60*, 60
Liquid ingredients, measuring, 130

M
Maple-Buttermilk Cake, 118
Maple-Pecan Cake, *116*, 118
Marble Cake, 149
Margarine, about, 131
Marigolds, how to make, *141*, 141
Marzipan Torte, 126, *127*
Measuring spoons, using, 130
Meringue Cake, 120
    lemon, 120, *121*
Mincemeat Fruitcake, 124
Mini Bûche de Noël Cakes, *54*, 55
Mocha Cream Torte, 122, *123*
Monkey Cake, *34*, 35, 36
Mother's Day Straw Hat Cake, 100–101, *101*
Mouse, cheese and, cake, *22*, 23

N
Nut(s)
    chocolate-dipped, 114
    white, cake, 113
Nutmeg Cake, 112
    custard-filled, *110*, 112

O
Orange-Coconut Cake, 150

P
Panda Cake, 38, *39*
Party blowers, 61
Pastel Marble Cake, 149
Peanut butter frosting, 151
Pecan, maple-, cake, *116*, 118
Penuche frosting, easy, 152

INDEX

Peppermint Chiffon Cake, 128

Peppermint Whipped Cream Cake, 56, 57

Petal tips, *139*, 139

Petits Fours, *89*, 89
   glaze, 153

Pinecone, holiday, cake, *50*, 52

Play Ball Cake, 40, *41*

Poppy seed, lemon-, cake, 150

Pot-o'-Gold Cake, 68–69, *69*

Pound Cake, 148
   golden, 127

Pumpkin-Gingerbread Cake, 148

Q

Quilt, holiday, cake, *56*, 56

R

Raspberry Sauce, 117

Reverse shell border, *140*, 140

Ribbons, chocolate, 144

Rope border, *140*, 140

Rose designs
   apricot, 88
   gumdrop, 88
   how to make, *141*, 141
   sugared, 88

Rosettes
   making, *138*, 138
   whipped cream, 88

S

Sailboat Cake, *42*, 43

"Seizing", definition of, 143

Shell border, *140*, 140

Shoe, athletic, cake, 11, *12*

Shortening, about, 131

Shower cakes
   baby bib, *94*, 94
   bootie, *94*, 95
   double-ring, 90–91, *91*

Skate, in-line, cake, 36–37, *37*

Snowman Cake, 25

Sour cream, cookie-, cake, 116

Spaceship Cake, 44, *45*

Specialty bakery cakes
   caramel, 114
   Caramel-Pecan Torte, 114, *115*
   chocolate cookie, *115*, 116
   Chocolate Mint Loaves, *127*, 128
   cookie-sour cream, 116
   custard-filled nutmeg, *111*, 112
   decadent chocolate, *116*, 117
   French silk hazelnut, *111*, 113
   Fruitcake Ring, 124, *125*
   Glazed Whole Wheat Fruitcake, 124, *125*
   golden pound, 127
   lemon meringue, 120, *121*
   maple-buttermilk, 118
   maple-pecan, *116*, 118
   Marzipan Torte, 126, *127*
   meringue, 120
   Mincemeat Fruitcake, 124
   Mocha Cream Torte, 122, *123*
   nutmeg, 112
   peppermint chiffon, 128
   strawberries and cream, 119, *121*
   Walnut Torte, 122, *123*
   whipped cream, 119
   white nut, 113

Spiderweb Cake, *74*, 74

Splitting cakes into layers, *134*, 134

Star of David Cake, 108, *109*

Star tips, *139*, 139

Stencil designs, 97

Storage tips
   cakes, 135
   chocolate, 143

Strawberries and Cream Cake, 119, *121*

Straw hat, Mother's Day, cake, 100–101, *101*

Swag border, *140*, 140

T

Teddy Bear Cake, 46, *47*

Thanksgiving Cake, *77*, 78

Tiered cake, yields, 85

Torte
   caramel-pecan, 114, *115*
   marzipan, 126, *127*
   walnut, 122, *123*

Train Cake, 48–49, *49*

Tree, Christmas, cake, 53, *54*

T-shirt, Father's Day, *102*, 102–3

Turkey Gobbler Cake, 76, *77*

Twigs, chocolate, 144

U

Umbrella Cake, 92, *93*

V

Vanilla frosting, creamy, 151

INDEX

W

Walnut Torte, 122, *123*

Whipped Cream Cake, 119

    peppermint and, *56*, 57

White Cake, 149

White chocolate glaze, 153

White decorator frosting, 152

White mountain frosting, 152

White Nut Cake, 113

Wild roses, how to make, *141*, 141

Writing tips, *139*, 139

Y

Yellow Cake, 150

Yields, cake, 85, 137

Z

Zigzag border, *140*, 140